THE ECOSYSTEM BUILDER'S PLAYBOOK

A PRACTICAL GUIDE TO RAPID LOCAL ECONOMIC TRANSFORMATION

Dr. Dell Gines, PhD, CEcD

Printed in the United States of America

Paperback ISBN: 978-1-965319-27-7

Purpose Publishing LLC.
13194 US Highway 301 South, Suite 417
Riverview, Florida 33578

www.PurposePublishing.com

TABLE OF CONTENTS

FORWARD

My journey into entrepreneurship ecosystem building began in March 2011 when I joined the Federal Reserve Bank of Kansas City. At the time, my boss asked what I hoped to accomplish in small business and economic development since it was the department's first effort. I told her that if we focused on the intersection of small business and economic development, we would become thought leaders within five years. That aspiration set me on a path filled with dedicated economic developers, inspiring entrepreneurship support organizations, and passionate ecosystem builders.

Over the years, I hosted two national conferences at the Federal Reserve, events that helped shape the conversation on entrepreneurship ecosystem building. My work involved convening thought leaders, speaking in more than 30 states and 60 cities, creating virtual courses, and offering guidance to organizations committed to entrepreneur-centered growth. Along the way, I was fortunate to collaborate with Network Kansas and develop a curriculum that became a certification program at the International Economic Development Council. Although these accomplishments felt significant, the real highlight was the people I met, many of whom were determined to uplift small towns, underserved neighborhoods, and overlooked populations through entrepreneurship.

It has been meaningful to support the economic development field by focusing on these ecosystems. I also pursued deeper study on the subject, which allowed me to examine the transformative power of entrepreneurship for communities that are often ignored or marginalized. I saw individuals willing to tackle inequality and empower new business creation everywhere I traveled. Their commitment affirmed my belief that real economic change starts with local entrepreneurs and grassroots advocates.

While I will continue to cheer on these efforts, this book represents my final formal work in entrepreneurship ecosystem building. I am shifting my focus to different economic development models and advancing projects in artificial intelligence for our field. As I wrap up this chapter in my career, I do so with gratitude and sadness. The last decade and a half has been filled with learning, collaboration, and friendship that forever shaped my perspective on growth and equity.

I hope you find practical insight and tangible value in these pages. More than anything, may this book encourage you to keep pushing the boundaries of what entrepreneurship can do in every corner of our communities. Thank you for reading and for doing the work that keeps our local economies thriving.

PRELUDE

Introduction

One thing stands out after fifteen years of working alongside ecosystem builders nationwide. These community changemakers have a bias toward action. This hands-on approach is inspiring but becomes most effective when guided by proven frameworks and strategies.

This prelude is your starting point if you share this urgency to impact your community. Think of it as a quick-start guide, a practical roadmap for your first three months of ecosystem building. These steps will help you focus your energy and build a strong foundation, pointing you toward deeper concepts throughout the book.

First Month: Building Your Foundation

- Form Your Initial Team (6-8 people). Gather a small, diverse group of committed individuals to kickstart your efforts.

- Map Existing Resources and Support Organizations. Identify the key assets in your community that support entrepreneurs.

- Interview 15-20 Local Entrepreneurs. Learn directly from business owners about their challenges and needs.

- Document Findings and Identify Priorities. Organize insights to determine where to focus your efforts.

Second Month: Creating Your First Project

- Choose a Focused, Achievable Initiative. Select a project that is both impactful and feasible.

- Build Key Relationships and Partnerships. Connect with stakeholders who can help make your project a success.

- Create Clear Success Metrics. Define how you will measure progress and outcomes.

- Set a 90-Day Action Plan. Outline specific steps and timelines to achieve your goals.

Third Month: Implementation and Learning

- Launch Your First Project. Put your plan into action and engage your community.

- Track Progress and Gather Feedback. Monitor what works and what needs adjustment.

- Document Lessons Learned. Record insights to improve future efforts.

- Plan Next Steps. Build on your success and identify what comes next.

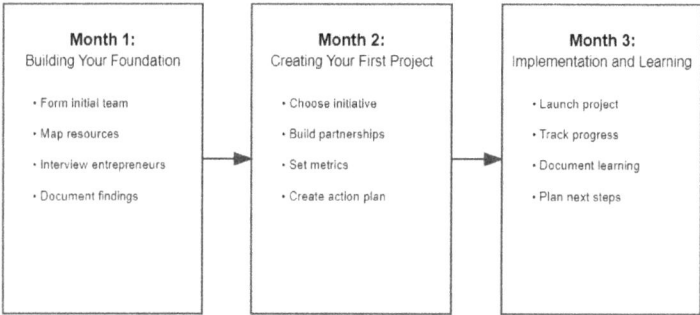

Month 1: Building Your Foundation	Month 2: Creating Your First Project	Month 3: Implementation and Learning
• Form initial team	• Choose initiative	• Launch project
• Map resources	• Build partnerships	• Track progress
• Interview entrepreneurs	• Set metrics	• Document learning
• Document findings	• Create action plan	• Plan next steps

Start Small. Think Systematically. Build Relationships. Document Everything.

Figure 1 - Minimum Viable Ecosystem Building Roadmap

Guiding Principles

- Start Small but Think Systematically. Begin with manageable projects while keeping the broader vision in mind.

- Focus on Building Relationships. Collaboration is crucial to creating a strong ecosystem.

- Document Everything You Learn. Insights from early actions will shape long-term success.

- Celebrate Early Wins. Recognize and share progress to sustain momentum.

- Share Progress Regularly. Keep stakeholders informed and engaged.

- Stay Flexible and Adapt as Needed. Be prepared to pivot based on feedback and results.

This roadmap is designed to give you direction without overloading you with details. For now, focus on assembling your initial team and reaching out to local entrepreneurs so you can learn directly from them.

Where to Look Next for Deeper Guidance

- Building Your Team: Chapter 13 explores how to gather and engage the best stakeholders for your initiative.

- Identifying and Supporting Entrepreneurs: Chapter 8 covers strategies for finding, connecting with, and assisting local business owners.

- Mapping Your Ecosystem: Chapter 11 explains how to visualize community resources and see how they fit together.

- Developing Your First Project: Chapter 14 guides you in turning your ideas into concrete, results-oriented actions.

- Measuring and Scaling Impact: Chapters 15 and 16 show how to expand your efforts and maintain success over time.

If you are ready to learn more, proceed to Chapter 1 for foundational ideas on why entrepreneurship matters and how bottom-up economic development can reshape your community. If you prefer to act immediately, start following the roadmap above and refer to the suggested chapters.

ECOSYSTEM BUILDING CONCEPTS

*"The people who are crazy enough to think they can
change the world are the ones who do."*
- Steve Jobs

Entrepreneurship is a powerful catalyst for community transformation, yet it requires a supportive environment to thrive. Part I covers foundational concepts so you can understand why ecosystems matter, how they function, and which stakeholders play pivotal roles. These chapters lay the groundwork by showing you how to view entrepreneurship as both an economic driver and a community-based movement, ensuring your ecosystem-building efforts start on firm footing.

The chapters in this section build knowledge step by step:

- Chapter 1: Introduction to Ecosystem Building

  Explains why entrepreneurship fuels local growth, how ecosystem building differs from traditional economic development, and why the bottom-up approach can spark sustained change.

- Chapter 2: A Deeper Dive Into Entrepreneurship Ecosystems

  Examines the interplay between personal assets like skills and finances and environmental factors such as policy and culture, revealing how systems thinking clarifies your path forward.

- Chapter 3: The Transparent Ecosystem

  Highlights the difference between fragmented resources and cohesive support networks. Shows how entrepreneurs benefit from reduced confusion and easier access to services.

- Chapter 4: Ecosystem Actors and Their Contributions

  Maps out the range of stakeholders, from local government and financial institutions to community organizations and non-traditional influencers. Emphasizes the value of collaboration and integrated partnerships.

- Chapter 5: The Role of the Entrepreneurship Ecosystem Builder

  Focuses on the individuals or organizations that act as connectors, advocates, and coordinators, ensuring the entire network remains aligned with the needs of local entrepreneurs.

By the end of Part I, you will have a comprehensive understanding of the key elements and players that make up a healthy, thriving entrepreneurship ecosystem. This foundation prepares you to move into more strategic and tactical approaches in the sections ahead.

CHAPTER 1

INTRODUCTION TO ECOSYSTEM BUILDING

Chapter Roadmap

In this chapter, you will learn:

- The Importance of Entrepreneurship and How It Drives Local Growth

- Why Ecosystem Building Matters More than Traditional Economic Development Methods

- How to Define an Entrepreneurship Ecosystem by Identifying Its Key Elements

- The Bottom-up Approach to Driving Meaningful, Lasting Change

- How Ecosystem Building Differs from Other Forms of Community Development

- A Preview of Next Steps so You Can Begin Transforming Your Own Community

Introduction

Across many communities, local entrepreneurs create new jobs, revitalize empty storefronts, and inspire residents to think creatively about what their hometown can achieve. By building successful businesses, these innovators improve local economies in ways that large outside corporations rarely do. At the same time, they cultivate a sense of ownership among the people who live there. Rather than depending on distant companies, communities that invest in local founders encourage a resilient, homegrown economy.

Yet, not all regions know how to nurture or sustain entrepreneurs. In some places, business owners struggle to locate the most basic support, such as funding or mentorship. This leads to missed opportunities, economic stagnation, and an ongoing sense that only a few lucky areas can enjoy the benefits of innovation.

Entrepreneurship ecosystem building addresses this problem. It offers a purposeful, community-centered strategy that helps entrepreneurs start and grow their businesses easily. This chapter explains why this method is so relevant and outlines how people in your community can adapt it. The goal is to show that if you invest in local entrepreneurs, you invest in your community's future. By the end of this chapter, you will understand the foundation of entrepreneurship ecosystem building and why it offers a hopeful path for sustainable local growth.

Why Does Entrepreneurship Ecosystem Building Matter?

Entrepreneurs are the main source of new jobs and wealth generation for many towns and cities. When a local startup succeeds, it hires from within the community, invests profits back into local services, and often collaborates with other small businesses. This multiplier effect benefits everyone, from schools to local retailers.

Conventional economic development often focuses on attracting large corporations through tax breaks or similar incentives. While that may bring short-term job growth, it can also leave communities vulnerable if the company decides to relocate or cut staff. Entrepreneurship ecosystem building takes a more grassroots approach by fostering local talent. This helps communities maintain control over their economic future and adapt more quickly when challenges arise.

Another benefit is inclusivity. Traditional development deals often focus on large industries or a narrow slice of the population. Building a robust entrepreneurship ecosystem gives people from different backgrounds and skill sets a path to success. It encourages diversity, which fuels new ideas and unlocks a wider range of entrepreneurial talent.

Defining Entrepreneurship Ecosystems

In an entrepreneurship ecosystem, everyone works together to make starting a business more accessible and efficient. Think of it like a garden. You need fertile soil, water, sunlight, and care to help plants flourish. In this analogy, entrepreneurs are the seeds, and the ecosystem is the environment that supports their growth.

Below are the six core elements of an entrepreneurship ecosystem. These elements should connect and reinforce each other:

1. Entrepreneurial Skills: Skills refer to practical know-how. Entrepreneurs need knowledge in finance, operations, marketing, and team leadership. They often develop these abilities through education, training, or direct experience. Ecosystems that offer workshops, accelerators, or mentorship help founders refine these skills.

2. Relationships: Vibrant ecosystems rely on supportive networks. Entrepreneurs thrive when they can learn from each other, access mentors, or connect with investors and potential partners. These relationships spark new ideas and help founders solve problems more quickly.

3. Finances: Capital is critical for startups and growing businesses. This includes personal funds, loans from local banks, angel investments, grants, or crowdfunding. An ecosystem that provides a variety of funding sources ensures that entrepreneurs can find the right financing at each growth stage.

4. Culture: Communities that reward innovation, celebrate entrepreneurship, and treat failure as a learning opportunity encourage more people to pursue their own ventures. Frequent meetups, local success stories, and public support for entrepreneurs can boost morale and spark new ideas across the community.

5. Policy: Policy sets the rules of the game. This includes local regulations, startup incentives, and the ease of getting permits. Entrepreneur-friendly policies reduce barriers and make it simpler for small businesses to focus on growing instead of navigating unnecessary red tape.

6. Physical and Digital Infrastructure: Founders need reliable internet, functional roads, and suitable workspaces to run their businesses effectively. Shared work areas, co-work spaces, or business incubators also foster networking and collaboration. Robust digital tools, such as online marketplaces or e-commerce platforms, further expand a venture's reach.

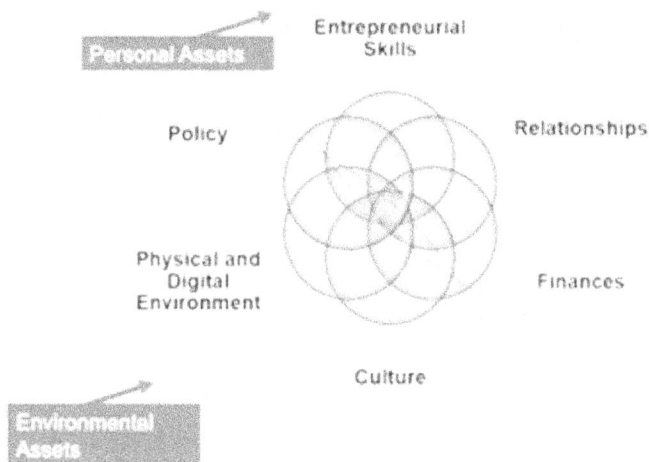

Personal Assets

Entrepreneurial
Skills

Policy

Relationships

Physical and
Digital
Environment

Finances

Culture

Environmental
Assets

Figure 2 - Six Elements of the Entrepreneurship Ecosystem

When these six elements come together in a balanced way, they form a strong ecosystem that helps entrepreneurs launch companies and sustains those businesses over time. All of this rests on collaboration among local leaders, service providers, educators, and, of course, entrepreneurs themselves.

Understanding the Bottom-up Approach to Economic Development

Entrepreneurship ecosystem building focuses on local people and organizations taking the lead. Instead of relying heavily on outside investment or external programs, the bottom-up approach recognizes that people who live in the community have the clearest sense of its challenges and potential.

This does not mean ignoring outside expertise or partnerships. It means that plans and decisions start with local viewpoints. By honoring local knowledge, communities can design solutions that fit their specific culture and resources. These efforts often grow gradually through shared projects like small business meetups or community-supported microloans, leading to more sustainable outcomes than programs led by external entities.

Examples of Bottom-up Action

- Neighborhood Resource Hubs: Residents work together to open small coworking spaces and host training sessions for new entrepreneurs.

- Peer Mentoring Networks: Established business owners volunteer a few hours monthly to guide newcomers, build trust, and share local market wisdom.

- Local Investment Groups: Groups of citizens pool funds to invest in promising area startups, keeping financial returns within the community.

These bottom-up activities encourage collaboration and shared ownership. The result is an ecosystem that responds to local needs, adapts to changes, and taps into existing strengths, ultimately leading to more inclusive, long-lasting growth.

Conclusion

Entrepreneurship ecosystem building is a fresh way to grow a community from the inside out. By uniting stakeholders, aligning resources, and encouraging local leaders, communities can foster environments that help entrepreneurs succeed. This chapter describes why entrepreneurs matter, the basics of entrepreneurship ecosystems, and how a bottom-up approach amplifies local potential.

As you advance through this book, you will explore practical tactics for applying these principles in your area. From mapping assets to launching early projects, the upcoming chapters provide tools to help you shape an innovative and resilient system. By committing to this approach, you invest in more than individual businesses. You invest in a prosperous, thriving future for all who call your community home.

CHAPTER 2

A DEEPER DIVE INTO ENTREPRENEURSHIP ECOSYSTEMS

Chapter Roadmap

In this chapter, you will learn:

- Why Systems Thinking Helps Communities See the Bigger Picture of Their Ecosystem

- How Personal Assets like Skills and Relationships Interact with External Factors

- What Environmental Assets such as Culture, Infrastructure, and Policy Look like in Practice

- Why Interconnections Among Resources Determine the Ecosystem's Overall Health

- How to Recognize Gaps that Hinder Collaboration and Entrepreneurial Success

Introduction

As explained in Chapter 1, an entrepreneurial ecosystem depends on how people, resources, and organizations connect to help new or growing ventures. This chapter expands on the importance of a systems-thinking approach and examines how personal and environmental factors affect an entrepreneur's path. You will also see how strong connections among these factors benefit local businesses and drive broader community progress.

The Value of Systems Thinking in Entrepreneurship Support

Many communities create programs to support entrepreneurs, yet these often happen in isolation. Systems thinking provides a broader viewpoint by highlighting how different services and stakeholders can complement one another. For example, a local mentorship program can achieve a greater impact when it offers consistent referrals to training sessions or local loan providers.

Analyzing how each initiative influences others also reveals gaps or overlaps. Small changes, such as improved internet service or a recurring meetup for founders, can strengthen the entire support network when they are planned with the ecosystem's needs in mind. This approach leads to clearer pathways for entrepreneurs to get advice, funding, or specialized support.

Personal Assets in Entrepreneurship Ecosystems

As noted in Chapter 1, personal assets include skills, relationships, and finances. While these are distinct, they often reinforce each other.

- Skills: Founders need abilities in areas like financial planning, marketing, leadership, and product design. Communities bolster these skills with targeted workshops, webinars, or incubator programs that cover everything from writing a business plan to pitching a new product.

- Relationships: Entrepreneurs benefit from mentors, peer groups, or local leaders who can share expertise or introduce them to potential investors and clients. The more diverse these networks are, the easier for founders to discover unique insights or secure essential partnerships.

- Finances: Firms need enough capital to stay afloat and invest in growth. Funds may come from savings, banks, venture capital, or crowdfunding. When an ecosystem fosters transparent information about how to secure capital, entrepreneurs can find the right fit for their stage of growth and business model.

By strengthening these personal assets, communities help founders navigate from ideas to successful ventures more smoothly. This might include workshops in local colleges, targeted microloan programs, or resource-sharing groups that bring together established and emerging business owners.

Environmental Assets in Entrepreneurship Ecosystems

Environmental assets are the conditions that surround entrepreneurs. They include culture, infrastructure, and policy. Each factor affects how easily a person can launch and scale a business.

- Culture: A culture that values risk-taking and innovation makes entrepreneurship feel accessible. Celebrating local business achievements, publicizing success stories, or hosting periodic pitch nights contribute to a supportive atmosphere that draws in new founders.

- Infrastructure: Practical facilities, such as well-maintained roads and affordable office space, along with reliable digital tools, help businesses operate efficiently. Coworking sites or business incubators often spark collaboration and support. Even small details, like zoning that allows for mixed-use development, can impact how conveniently entrepreneurs can set up and run their ventures.

- Policy: Policies that reduce red tape and simplify permit processes can lighten the load on entrepreneurs. Local government support, like startup grants or tax incentives, can encourage more residents to try new ideas. Public programs that assist with regulatory compliance or licensing foster smoother growth for startups.

Strong environmental assets allow entrepreneurs to channel their time and energy into building their products or services. If these external factors are weak, founders spend too much time overcoming logistical barriers instead of innovating.

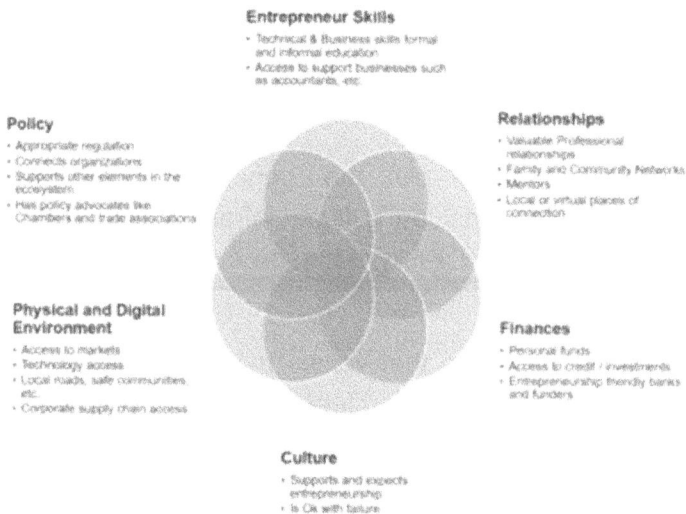

Figure 3 - Expanded Ecosystem

Interconnections and System Strength

Even if a community has many resources, the way these elements intersect can either boost or undermine entrepreneurs. A strong system is one where:

- Entrepreneurs can quickly learn about available support

- Service organizations share information about common clients or needs

- Stakeholders understand each other's roles and collaborate rather than overlap

If resources stay siloed, founders may not know how to access critical programs or experts. This can lead to gaps in funding, mentorship, or day-to-day guidance. Conversely, a connected ecosystem creates seamless pathways so entrepreneurs can move from initial ideas to tested ventures without needless delays. The result is a smoother, more transparent environment that welcomes a range of new businesses.

Conclusion

Entrepreneurship ecosystems blend personal assets, such as skills and finances, with supportive environmental factors, such as culture and policy. Systems thinking helps communities see how these parts fit together, revealing ways to strengthen weak links and encourage cross-pollination between programs or organizations. Whether you focus on improving digital infrastructure or creating mentorship circles, your efforts matter most when woven into a cohesive strategy.

In the chapters ahead, you will learn practical methods for mapping your local resources, identifying gaps, and forming teams to tackle real projects with maximum impact. By continuously refining and connecting personal and environmental assets, your community can boost innovation, lower barriers for new founders, and cultivate a lasting sense of collaborative growth.

CHAPTER 3

THE TRANSPARENT ECOSYSTEM: MOVING FROM FOGGY TO CLEAR

Chapter Roadmap

In this chapter, you will learn:

- How Fragmented Systems Make It Difficult for Entrepreneurs to Find Support

- What Sets Transparent Ecosystems Apart from Disjointed Ones

- Why Moving from Sparse to Dense Strengthens Collaboration and Resource-Sharing

- When Quality Matters More than the Sheer Number of Available Programs

- How to Apply These Insights for Practical Improvements

Introduction

Chapters 1 and 2 explained the fundamentals of entrepreneurship ecosystems and why a systems-thinking approach is crucial. Despite having resources, many communities struggle because entrepreneurs find those resources scattered or confusing. They encounter multiple programs and services, yet cannot easily link them to their specific needs. This disconnect results in lost time and missed opportunities.

In this chapter, you will see how ecosystems can move away from fragmented and isolated resources. By focusing on clarity and connection, communities reduce the "fog" that keeps entrepreneurs from thriving. Whether it involves simplifying access points, creating shared networks, or shifting from a thin spread of resources to more robust offerings, the goal is to make it straightforward for founders to get the help they need.

From Fragmented to Connected

A fragmented entrepreneurial system exists when organizations, financial institutions, incubators, and training programs operate without coordination. Entrepreneurs often struggle to figure out where to start. They may rely on personal connections or happenstance to learn about new funding options, business workshops, or mentorship opportunities.

A connected system, however, brings stakeholders together to share information, align services, and streamline referrals. For example, an economic development organization might partner with local banks and accelerator programs to offer unified onboarding for aspiring founders. Instead of forcing individuals to hunt through multiple listings or websites, the connected system immediately guides them to the relevant resources.

Characteristics of a Fragmented System

- Unclear entry points
- Isolated support services
- Limited information sharing
- High barriers to navigation
- Inconsistent communication

Characteristics of a Connected System

- Shared knowledge across organizations
- Joint problem-solving and referrals
- Standardized communication channels
- Greater visibility of available programs
- Coordinated efforts that reduce redundancy

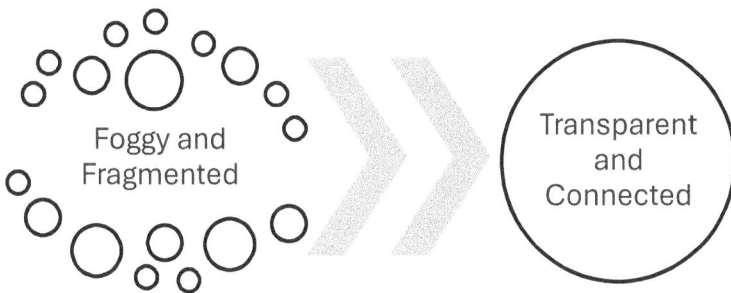

Figure 4 - From Foggy to Transparent Ecosystems

Shifting from fragmentation to connection helps entrepreneurs spend more time refining their businesses and less time searching for fragmented sources of help. For those looking to take the next step, Chapter 2's emphasis on systems thinking can guide you in building the partnerships and referral networks needed to unify local resources.

Moving from Sparse to Dense

Some communities do not have enough programs or providers to serve the spectrum of entrepreneurial needs. This results in a sparse environment where entrepreneurs can access only one or two forms of support. Others may have many service providers, yet they remain underutilized or disorganized. In such cases, the ecosystem is "foggy" because individuals are unaware of everything available.

By contrast, a dense ecosystem has multiple, interconnected organizations offering diverse forms of assistance. Entrepreneurs might find training sessions, pitch events, networking nights, specialized loan programs, or incubators all supported by an underlying culture of collaboration. Chapter 1 mentioned how a vibrant culture encourages entrepreneurship. Here, we see that abundant and accessible resources further boost this positive environment.

Strategies to Move from Sparse to Dense

- Expand Partnerships: Collaborate with nearby communities or regional hubs. If your immediate area lacks certain support services, partnering with a neighboring city's accelerator or coworking space may bridge the gap.

- Leverage Virtual Options: When local resources are limited, online meetups, digital incubator programs, or remote mentorship platforms can help entrepreneurs connect with experts outside their immediate region.

- Refine Communication: A centralized website, social media group, or email newsletter can highlight upcoming workshops or funding opportunities so entrepreneurs do not miss key events.

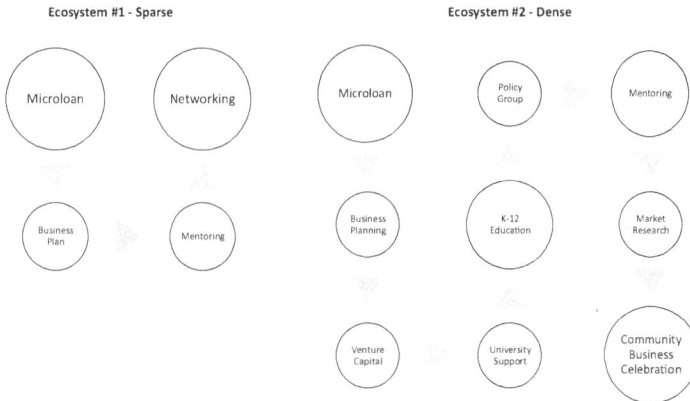

Ecosystem #1 - Sparse

Microloan Networking

Business Plan Mentoring

Ecosystem #2 - Dense

Microloan Policy Group Mentoring

Business Planning K-12 Education Market Research

Venture Capital University Support Community Business Celebration

Figure 5 - Sparse to Dense Ecosystems

Quality Over Quantity

Having numerous programs does not always lead to better results. Entrepreneurs still face roadblocks if workshops repeat the same basic topics or do not attract experienced mentors. A few well-structured, high-impact initiatives can outshine a long list of general offerings that lack clarity or measurable outcomes.

- Ensure Cultural Relevance: A Saturday seminar at a local library might be convenient for one group but not for entrepreneurs who need evening events after store-closing hours. Tailor programs to accommodate real schedules and lifestyles.

- Vet Service Providers: Confirm that each organization or individual offering support has subject-matter expertise and the ability to connect with diverse groups effectively.

- Promote Accessibility: Cost, timing, language barriers, and transportation gaps can hamper participation. Streamlined online content or recorded sessions let entrepreneurs access resources on their schedule.

Focusing on a handful of solid programs in many ecosystems leads to better engagement than spreading limited resources across many disconnected initiatives.

Implications for Ecosystem Building

When entrepreneurs spend more time figuring out how to reach resources than using them, the ecosystem wastes potential. On the other hand, a transparent and well-connected environment frees founders to concentrate on product development, customer engagement, or scaling strategies. This boosts individual ventures and the community's overall economic growth.

Cultivating a transparent system often begins with the following:

- Centralized Directories: Keep an updated catalog of support services, mentors, and funding sources.

- Regular Coordination: Host monthly or quarterly stakeholder meetings to compare notes and refine referral processes.

- Shared Data: If permitted, create ways for organizations to share anonymized data about common client needs, which can spark collaborative problem solving.

- Community Engagement: Encourage feedback from entrepreneurs about program effectiveness or missed resources, then adjust accordingly.

A transparent ecosystem reduces friction, encourages repeated collaboration, and helps every participant see their role in the larger network.

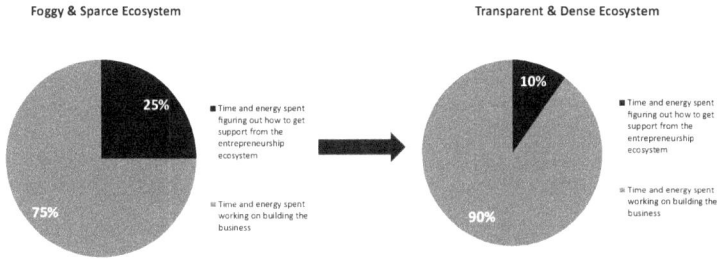

Foggy & Sparce Ecosystem

25%

■ Time and energy spent figuring out how to get support from the entrepreneurship ecosystem

75%

■ Time and energy spent working on building the business

Transparent & Dense Ecosystem

10%

■ Time and energy spent figuring out how to get support from the entrepreneurship ecosystem

90%

■ Time and energy spent working on building the business

Figure 6 - Benefits to Entrepreneurs of Moving to a Transparent and Dense Ecosystem

Conclusion

Communities can have abundant resources and still fail to help entrepreneurs if those resources remain isolated or hidden. Moving from a foggy, fragmented system to a transparent, well-connected environment involves clarifying entry points, coordinating existing programs, and making purposeful decisions about which services to expand or strengthen.

The result is an ecosystem where founders spend their time growing their businesses instead of struggling to find help. By focusing on clarity, density, and quality, you prepare your community to support entrepreneurs at every stage. In the following chapters, we will further explore tactics for mapping resources, building cohesive teams, and taking strategic action so you can sustain this positive momentum.

CHAPTER 4

ECOSYSTEM ACTORS AND THEIR CONTRIBUTIONS

Chapter Roadmap

In this chapter, you will learn:

- Which Stakeholders Commonly Participate in Entrepreneurship Ecosystems

- How Stakeholders Contribute Unique Resources and Perspectives

- Why Relationship-Building Anchors Every Ecosystem-Building Effort

- Ways to Collaborate More Effectively Among Different Groups

- How to Move from Silos to Integrated Systems That Boost Entrepreneur Success

Introduction

Entrepreneurship ecosystems thrive when many different stakeholders collaborate to support founders. As mentioned in Chapter 3, a connected ecosystem benefits everyone. However, reaching that level of cooperation depends on ensuring that both traditional and non-traditional key actors are recognized, included, and mobilized around shared goals.

In this chapter, we explore these stakeholders' diverse roles and strengths, ranging from local banks and educational institutions to community organizers and faith leaders. We then discuss fostering strong relationships and shifting from siloed efforts to a more integrated approach.

Who Will Be Involved in Ecosystem Building

Ecosystems succeed when organizations and individuals from different backgrounds come together. These stakeholders often include:

Actor	Definition
Economic Development Organizations	Coordinate essential support services for entrepreneurs (training, mentoring, etc.). Manage business assistance programs (grants, incubators, etc.). Connect entrepreneurs to resources (funding, facilities, etc.). Foster collaboration among support entities. Track ecosystem progress and refine approaches.
Financial Institutions	Provide access to capital (loans, lines of credit, etc.). Offer financial education. Participate in gap financing. Act as referral partners. Share expertise on financial trends.

Small Business Support Organizations	Provide targeted assistance (product development, supply chain management, etc.). Help with business planning and market research. Offer export guidance. Simplify regulatory compliance.
Educational Institutions	Prepare future entrepreneurs (courses, certifications, degrees). Conduct research and provide technical expertise. Offer facilities and resources (labs, coworking spaces, etc.). Align workforce development with local needs.
Local Government	Develop entrepreneur-friendly policies (tax incentives, zoning regulations, etc.). Oversee regulatory practices. Invest in infrastructure (broadband, transportation, etc.). Allocate resources to entrepreneurship initiatives. Partner with organizations to implement programs.
Business Leaders and Entrepreneurs	Share practical insights and act as mentors. Identify gaps in the ecosystem. Pilot new initiatives. Foster a collaborative culture through peer support.
Community Organizations	Build networks and connect stakeholders. Organize workshops, networking sessions, and expos. Advocate for entrepreneurship. Link businesses to the community (customers, partners, etc.).
Individual Ecosystem Builders	Act as trusted connectors and foster collaboration. Activate local resources. Inspire energy around entrepreneurship. Maintain momentum through strong relationships.

When these different groups collaborate, entrepreneurs gain access to a robust range of knowledge and support, which helps them solve problems more quickly and grow more confidently.

Stakeholders' Unique Contributions

Each stakeholder group offers specialized value:

- Expertise: Business leaders, educators, and technical advisors provide the know-how entrepreneurs need to navigate a new market or product category.

- Resources: Financial institutions supply capital, community organizations share physical meeting spaces, and local government may offer grant funding or incentives.

- Networks: Mentors and industry groups connect founders with potential customers, suppliers, or investors.

- Advocacy: Faith leaders and activists help highlight policy changes needed to make the ecosystem more equitable.

- Research and Data: Colleges or universities study trends, conduct focus groups, and measure program outcomes, which informs future decision-making.

Traditional Stakeholders	Non-Traditional Stakeholders
Community members	Community activists
Local business owners	Social justice leaders
Neighborhood leaders	Advocacy groups
Engaged citizens	Reform champions
Community organizers	Bottom-up organizers

Bankers	Other leaders (e.g., thought leaders, philanthropists)
Commercial lenders	Arts/culture leaders (e.g., museum directors, artists)
Credit union leaders	Education officials (e.g., school board members, teachers)
Investment managers	Media representatives (e.g., journalists, bloggers)
Financial advisors	Youth advocates
Entrepreneurs	Environmental groups
Startup founders	Historic preservation societies
Main Street owners	Public health officials
Tech entrepreneurs	Researchers (e.g., university faculty, think tanks)
Social entrepreneurs	Social service providers
Economic developers	Neighborhood associations
Chamber leaders	Community foundations
City/county staff	Labor unions
Business recruiters	Real estate developers
Workforce developers	Transportation planners

This alignment of varied strengths creates a supportive environment that addresses many facets of starting and running a business. Without such collective effort, entrepreneurs would rely on scattered, uncoordinated resources.

Building Relationships in Your Ecosystem

Strong relationships are at the heart of any ecosystem-building effort. Chapter 2 introduced the idea that stronger connections foster better outcomes. This is especially true for stakeholder collaboration because most services and benefits emerge from trusted connections.

Key Relationship Types

- Organization-to-Organization: A chamber of commerce might work with a local credit union to offer small-business workshops. Coordinating scheduling and goals ensures entrepreneurs receive financial advice and market insights in a single program.

- Entrepreneur-to-Entrepreneur: Peer support networks give founders safe spaces to share ideas, troubleshoot common challenges, and celebrate milestones. These relationships often extend beyond formal meetings, creating a sense of camaraderie.

- Supporter-to-Entrepreneur: Nonprofit staff, bankers, and educators can offer referrals or direct assistance to founders. Maintaining open lines of communication helps everyone stay informed about current programs, new funding options, or upcoming community events.

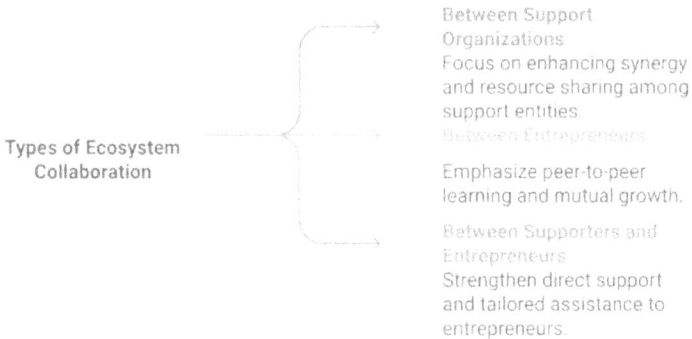

Types of Ecosystem Collaboration

Between Support Organizations
Focus on enhancing synergy and resource sharing among support entities.

Between Entrepreneurs
Emphasize peer-to-peer learning and mutual growth.

Between Supporters and Entrepreneurs
Strengthen direct support and tailored assistance to entrepreneurs.

Figure 6 - Types of Ecosystem Relationships

Practical Steps to Building Collaborative Networks

- Start with Clear Goals: Decide specific objectives for each partnership or initiative. This might involve boosting the number of women-owned businesses or expanding local export capacity.

- Promote Regular Engagement: Host monthly coffee events or short digital meetups so stakeholders can keep each other updated. Regular contact solidifies trust and encourages further collaboration.

- Create a Shared Directory or Online Hub: Many communities use a shared spreadsheet or website to list mentors, lenders, or training providers. This helps founders and partners quickly locate what they need.

- Measure Collaboration: Track outcomes, such as the number of joint events or referrals. Evaluate whether entrepreneurs find the support they need without excessive handoffs or confusion.

Moving from Silos to Systems

Many organizations, even those with strong missions, can inadvertently remain siloed. When programs overlap or operate in isolation, entrepreneurs waste time repeating their background information. They also miss out on combined benefits that might emerge from a more unified approach.

Shifting to a system mindset involves consistent information sharing, clearly defined responsibilities, and a culture of team-based problem-solving. Chapter 3 emphasized how clarity in access points helps entrepreneurs thrive. The same principle applies to stakeholder collaboration. By clarifying who does what, you make it easier for founders to receive help and reduce wasted effort among service providers.

Conclusion

Entrepreneurship ecosystems run on the collective efforts of diverse stakeholders, each with unique experiences, assets, and networks. These actors can multiply their impact by developing trusting relationships and aligning their programs. Instead of scattered projects that entrepreneurs struggle to navigate, you can create a connected system that nurtures businesses across all stages of growth.

In the following chapters, you will deepen your understanding of how to organize and implement strategic actions. From forming dedicated teams to managing ongoing initiatives, you will see how stakeholders pool their strengths for the benefit of local founders and the community as a whole.

THE ROLE OF
THE ENTREPRENEURSHIP
ECOSYSTEM BUILDER

Chapter Roadmap

In this chapter, you will learn:

- Who Ecosystem Builders Are and Why They Matter

- How Relationship Building Remains a Foundational Skill

- Why Navigating Conflicts and Championing Inclusivity Are Critical Tasks

- What Responsibilities Define an Ecosystem Builder's Day-to-Day Work

- How to Sustain Motivation and Momentum in the Ecosystem

Introduction

Previous chapters explained how different stakeholders and resources come together to support founders. One question remains: who ensures everyone coordinates and pushes the ecosystem forward? Enter the ecosystem builder.

Ecosystem builders are the connectors and organizers who look at the big picture. They see gaps in resources and take steps to fill them, encourage collaboration among diverse groups, and keep track of progress so the community can learn and improve. By guiding the work of other stakeholders, ecosystem builders help transform ideas about local entrepreneurship into sustainable action.

Defining Ecosystem Builders

Ecosystem builders can be individuals or entire organizations that champion the growth of local entrepreneurship. Their roles may vary, but they share common traits:

- Connector: They unite stakeholders from different sectors, such as banks, local government, educational institutions, and community groups, ensuring that entrepreneurs have a clear path to the support they need.

- Catalyst: They spot opportunities for new programs or partnerships and inspire people to get involved. If a local bank has funds for small loans, the ecosystem builder might connect that bank with a mentoring group or a business incubator, so founders benefit from capital and guidance.

- Facilitators: They run workshops, host networking events, and lead discussions that maintain a spirit of collaboration and trust. Their work ensures that stakeholders communicate regularly and share information.

- Advocate: They represent entrepreneurs' interests to policymakers, civic leaders, or larger funding bodies. When they see a common obstacle, they speak up to promote policies or resources to solve the problem.

By performing these tasks, ecosystem builders help local ventures progress from initial ideas to established businesses.

The Central Role of Relationship Building

All the connectors, catalysts, and facilitators described above depend on strong relationships. These relationships center on trust, which does not emerge overnight. Whether introducing an established company to a startup or bringing a local foundation together with volunteer mentors, ecosystem builders must earn each participant's confidence.

Keys to Relationship Building

- Listen Actively: Take time to hear stakeholders' concerns and needs. This helps you tailor your approach and shows respect for their perspectives.

- Be Transparent: Communicate your goals, progress, and challenges openly. If people sense hidden agendas, it is harder for them to commit fully.

- Foster Mutual Benefit: Show how each stakeholder gains from joining the network. This can be new clients, shared costs, or a stronger community brand.

- Maintain Regular Contact: Use consistent check-ins, events, or online tools so participants remain engaged and can see incremental wins.

When relationships are nurtured patiently and inclusively, stakeholders trust the ecosystem builder's guidance and become more receptive to working together.

Navigating Challenges

Ecosystem builders often stand in the middle of conflicting interests, resource limitations, or personality differences. They must handle these tensions diplomatically.

- Mediating Competition: Organizations might compete for the same grants or clients, so entrepreneurs receive mixed messages. The ecosystem builder can highlight mutually beneficial partnerships or ways to differentiate services.

- Balancing Diverse Perspectives: Some groups focus on serving high-tech startups, while others champion neighborhood microbusinesses. An ecosystem builder ensures each audience finds relevant support and sees how the community benefits from variety.

- Addressing Systemic Barriers: Underrepresented groups often do not have equal access to resources. Advocating for inclusive policies and targeted programs can help. An ecosystem builder who remains vigilant about equity can broaden opportunities for everyone.

- Overcoming Siloed Mindsets: As mentioned in Chapter 4, silos form when stakeholders fail to collaborate. An ecosystem builder fosters a culture of sharing, addresses trust issues, and creates joint projects that unite partners under shared objectives.

By identifying potential tensions early, ecosystem builders help minimize friction and keep the ecosystem on a steady growth path.

Core Responsibilities of an Ecosystem Builder

Although every community's needs differ, most ecosystem builders share key responsibilities:

- Strategic Planning: They set priorities and timelines, often informed by earlier mapping exercises or feedback sessions with entrepreneurs.

- Program Coordination: They track workshops, mentoring sessions, funding opportunities, and more, ensuring that events or services align with the ecosystem's overall vision.

- Monitoring and Evaluation: They document data on program usage, stakeholder engagement, and entrepreneurial outcomes, then analyze these results to refine strategies. Chapter 2 emphasizes the importance of a systems perspective, which means checking that each effort bolsters rather than duplicates others.

- Communication and Outreach: They maintain connections with local media, civic groups, and online platforms to spread news about programs or successes. Visibility encourages more founders to take advantage of resources.

- Resource Mobilization: They seek grants, sponsorships, or partnerships that fill gaps in funding, professional expertise, or space. This may involve writing proposals, cultivating donors, or working with local banks.

These responsibilities evolve over time, especially as the community changes or new partners emerge, so ecosystem builders must remain flexible.

Conclusion

Ecosystem builders hold a vital and multi-faceted role. They connect the dots between people, programs, and policy, ensuring entrepreneurs experience a cohesive network of support rather than a patchwork of isolated resources. Through relationship building, conflict management, and continuous coordination, they maintain the ecosystem's momentum and guard against fragmentation.

The following sections of this book dive deeper into how-to design and implement effective strategies for ecosystem growth. From forming specialized working groups to rolling out new projects, each effort benefits from an ecosystem builder's guidance. By uniting the community around a shared vision, ecosystem builders make entrepreneurship more accessible and foster a culture that values local innovation.

ECOSYSTEM BUILDING STRATEGY

"The best way to predict the future is to create it together."
- Abraham Lincoln

Learning the core ideas of entrepreneurship ecosystems is only the start. Part II moves from foundational concepts to practical strategies that help you design and implement meaningful work. Focusing on methods to narrow efforts, set clear milestones, and keep momentum, you transform high-level insights into actionable plans that serve entrepreneurs and strengthen your community.

These chapters guide you through a systematic approach:

- Chapter 6: From Concept to Strategy

  Explores how to pinpoint priorities, achieve early wins, and build a roadmap that balances short-term action with long-term goals.

- Chapter 7: Discover, Define, Develop, Do Action Framework

  Introduces the Double Diamond method, adapted for ecosystem building, to help you uncover challenges, set goals, design solutions, and implement plans.

- Chapter 8: Discovery – Identifying Your Entrepreneurs

  Shows how to locate and connect with specific groups of founders, using people- and place-based approaches to target real needs.

- Chapter 9: Discovery – Qualitative

  Explains how to use focus groups, interviews, and surveys to understand the human stories behind local businesses. Highlights why personal insights improve decision-making.

- Chapter 10: Discovery – Quantitative Data

  Demonstrates where to find numerical indicators of local trends, from government reports to commercial databases, and how to integrate them with your qualitative findings.

- Chapter 11: Discover – Understanding Your Ecosystem

  Introduces mapping techniques to visualize resources, connections, and possible gaps. Combines asset mapping with ecosystem mapping for a complete picture of your community.

- Chapter 12: Bridging Insights to Action

  Explains how to consolidate your discoveries, conduct a SWOT analysis, and decide which paths to pursue. Emphasizes sharing and validating findings with stakeholders for buy-in.

By the end of Part II, you will have a clear roadmap for gathering the right data, targeting the right entrepreneurs, and setting up organized initiatives. This section prepares you to move on to Part III, where you will learn how to form teams, develop specific projects, and maintain long-term progress.

CHAPTER 6

FROM CONCEPT TO STRATEGY

Chapter Roadmap

In this chapter, you will learn:

- Why It Is Important to Focus Your Efforts Despite Ecosystem Complexity

- How Early Wins Build Momentum for Long-Term Growth

- Why Timelines Matter and How to Plan Them Effectively

- What Tools You Can Use to Keep Your Strategy on Track

- How to Maintain Ongoing Energy and Progress

Introduction

Earlier chapters explained what ecosystem building involves and who participates in it. Many communities now realize they need a practical roadmap to turn ideas into concrete steps. That is where strategy enters. A deliberate, well-aligned plan steers your ecosystem from a collection of resources to a cohesive movement that empowers local entrepreneurs.

This chapter presents principles for bridging the gap between broad concepts and tangible outcomes. You can move with purpose by narrowing your focus, achieving early wins, and keeping an eye on timelines. You will also learn how to organize your next few months in a way that sustains motivation among stakeholders.

Narrowing the Focus

Entrepreneurship ecosystems often feel overwhelming because there are many parts, such as funding, training programs, networking events, partnerships, and more. Without a clear focus, groups can spend time on activities that do not lead to measurable change. To avoid that, you can:

- Map the Full Landscape: Start by revisiting your community's resource mapping (Chapter 11 will cover this in-depth) to see every available program or partner.

- Pick Key Priorities: Identify one or two major gaps or opportunities instead of fixing everything at once. It might be developing a mentorship network or creating an online portal that lists local funding resources.

- Set Boundaries: Clarify what is within your current capacity. If you lack the finances or workforce to expand citywide, focus on one neighborhood or a specific demographic.

This approach does not ignore the larger vision. It lets you concentrate on a few initiatives that can show progress quickly, encouraging more partners to join.

Creating Early Wins

Long timelines without visible results often cause stakeholder fatigue. Demonstrating progress within three to six months shows people that ecosystem building pays off. These "early wins" might be:

- Launching a Low-Cost Pilot: For example, a short series of free workshops for entrepreneurs held at a local library.

- Establishing a New Partnership: Perhaps your organization teams up with a regional bank to co-host a business pitch event.

- Securing a Small Grant: Even a modest amount of outside funding validates your efforts and can be used to seed microloans or sponsor a meetup.

Publicize these successes to remind the community that positive change is happening. Sharing photos, short testimonials, or data points on social media or in newsletters keeps stakeholders engaged.

Timeline Considerations

A plan that spans several months or a year should outline how and when each key activity will happen. For instance:

1. Immediate (First 30 Days)
   - Form an action team
   - Set clear objectives
   - Outline target participants or demographics

2. Short Term (1-3 Months)
   - Initiate a pilot project
   - Host a simple community event
   - Collect early feedback

3. Medium Term (3-6 Months)

   o Evaluate results of pilot

   o Refine or expand successful elements

   o Pursue additional funding or partnerships

4. Long Term (6-12 Months)

   o Scale up effective programs

   o Share lessons and data

   o Introduce new strategies based on feedback

This rolling structure helps maintain steady momentum. Each period should end with a brief check-in. This keeps everyone alert to lessons learned and allows you to set new or revised goals based on real progress.

Maintaining Momentum

A plan by itself does not ensure action. Many projects stall after a big kickoff event. To prevent this, use these strategies:

- Regular Communication: Send monthly updates highlighting successes and next steps. Use a simple format that focuses on specific tasks completed and upcoming goals.

- Assign Accountability: Make sure each task has an owner who commits to meeting deadlines. This prevents confusion and shared responsibility that can lead to delays.

- Celebrate Milestones: Acknowledge accomplishments such as a new partnership or a successful pilot. Even small victories can rejuvenate team spirit.

- Adapt as Needed: Track key metrics and make changes if something is not working. Ecosystem building requires agility. Rather than forcing a failing program to continue, reevaluate the approach and pivot.

By maintaining these habits, you empower your team to push forward, confident that each month or quarter brings new achievements and learning.

Conclusion

Moving from concept to strategy involves more than just deciding what to do. It means pinpointing clear priorities, achieving quick wins to build momentum, outlining timelines, and sustaining the energy needed to see projects through. This process keeps you from getting stuck in a planning cycle without real progress. As you build out your strategies, remember the lessons from earlier chapters about shared vision and diverse collaboration, then harness this momentum to bring your community's entrepreneurial aspirations to life.

CHAPTER 7

DISCOVER, DEFINE, DEVELOP, DO ACTION FRAMEWORK

Chapter Roadmap

In this chapter, you will learn:

- Where Design Thinking First Came From and How It Evolved

- What the Double Diamond Framework Is and Why It Helps Ecosystem Builders

- How the Four Phases Guide You From Problem Identification to Real-World Action

- Why This Method Fits Well With Local Ecosystem-Building Goals

- Where to Find Specific Tactics for Each Phase

Introduction

Many communities struggle to move from abstract discussions about entrepreneurship to concrete steps that foster genuine results. While previous chapters explored the importance of setting priorities and aiming for quick wins, you may still wonder how to organize this work, so it remains purposeful and adaptable. The "Double Diamond" method, initially a design thinking concept, offers a structured approach that fits well with the dynamic nature of local ecosystems.

This chapter explains why the Double Diamond method, adapted as Discover, Define, Develop, and Do, helps teams handle complex problems. By following a clear but flexible path, your group can align around shared goals, brainstorm practical solutions, test ideas early, and refine them for real impact.

Design Thinking's Double Diamond

Design thinking originated as a problem-solving method in the tech industry and product design. It highlighted the need to center on user needs, used creativity to propose solutions, and then refined them through rapid feedback. Over time, professionals outside technology noticed how well these principles could address broader community and economic challenges.

The Double Diamond is a visual representation of design thinking that encourages teams to explore issues widely, focus on specific challenges, brainstorm potential solutions, and finally choose a path for full implementation. This approach avoids jumping straight into solutions without proper understanding and prevents endless research without follow-up action.

Understanding the Double Diamond

The Double Diamond method is often described in two main phases: Problem Space and Solution Space. Each phase splits further into two steps, forming four stages that guide the team from initial research to tangible outcomes.

1. Discover: Gather broad insights. Talk to stakeholders, interview entrepreneurs, and observe current conditions. The idea is to open up possibilities rather than narrow them too soon.

2. Define: Identify the core challenges or opportunities from the information gathered. Distill your findings into precise, shared goals, making sure everyone knows what problem you plan to solve.

3. Develop: Brainstorm potential solutions or projects. Test early versions of your ideas, gather feedback, and refine them. Collaboration is key because it spurs creativity and new ideas.

4. Do: Implement the best solution, track its performance, and make iterative improvements. If necessary, pivot or adapt based on real-world results.

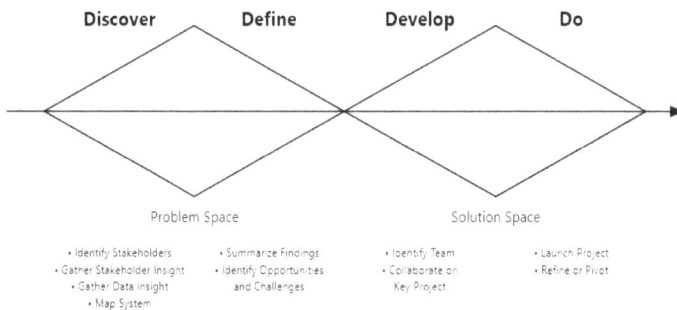

Figure 7 - Design Thinking for Ecosystem Builders

By separating discovery from solution design, teams avoid jumping to conclusions. By dedicating a final stage to action, they ensure that concepts do not linger in planning mode.

Why This Framework Works for Ecosystem Building

This method focuses on understanding community needs instead of assuming predefined solutions. It fits the bottom-up approach mentioned in earlier chapters because it actively involves local entrepreneurs, mentors, and organizations in shaping priorities.

- Structured Exploration: The Discover and Define steps align well with ecosystem mapping and interviews, as outlined in Chapters 2 and 3.

- Collaborative Design: The Develop step meshes with building strong stakeholder relationships, a theme that emerged in Chapters 4 and 5.

- Accountability to Action: The Do step supports strategic planning and quick wins, as introduced in Chapter 6.

This framework also encourages repeated iteration. The ecosystem must evolve so communities benefit from a cyclical process that regularly identifies challenges, tests solutions, and refines efforts.

The Four Phases in Detail

1. Discover

You begin by casting a wide net to gather information. Interview entrepreneurs, conduct focus groups, and collect data on local markets. Explore existing programs to see where overlaps or gaps occur. This mirrors how communities map their ecosystem or assess current strengths.

Key Tips

- Use surveys or community meetings to capture perspectives from multiple segments.

- Record recurring themes or barriers that keep surfacing.

- Remain open-minded about what the real issues might be.

2. Define

After you compile discoveries, meet with your team to identify common threads. If too many problems appear, choose one or two that are urgent and actionable. Define success by deciding how you will measure progress or evaluate results.

Key Tips

- Create a concise statement of the main problem.

- Check that all stakeholders understand and agree on the focus.

- Confirm which metrics matter most for tracking success.

3. Develop

In this stage, your team brainstorms multiple solutions, tests low-risk pilots, and revises them based on feedback. You can form smaller working groups specializing in particular fixes, such as a mentorship program or a small business fund.

Key Tips

- Encourage creativity by inviting various community members to share ideas.

- Start small with prototypes or pilot activities so you can learn quickly.

- Seek feedback early, not after you have sunk too many resources into a project.

4. Do

Finally, you launch your chosen initiative, monitor its progress, and refine as needed. This phase often includes planning events, opening new facilities, rolling out training sessions, or awarding micro-grants. Use clear timelines and assign responsibilities to maintain accountability.

Key Tips

- Set incremental goals that can be achieved within a few weeks or months.

- Track outcomes using simple metrics or regular check-ins with participants.

- Remain flexible; pivoting is allowed if the data shows a better path forward.

Conclusion

The Discover, Define, Develop, and Do framework empowers communities to address complicated challenges in an organized way. Instead of falling into planning paralysis or rushing into underinformed programs, you gather insights, identify priorities, generate practical solutions, and then put those ideas into practice. This approach aligns with the collaborative and adaptive nature of ecosystem building. In the upcoming chapters, you will see how each phase can be applied more specifically to researching local entrepreneurs, mapping community resources, and shaping effective interventions that bring genuine, long-term benefits.

CHAPTER 8

DISCOVERY – IDENTIFYING YOUR ENTREPRENEURS

Chapter Roadmap

In this chapter, you will learn:

- Why It Is Essential to Identify and Engage the Right Entrepreneurs in Your Community

- Ways to Target Specific Populations, Places, or a Combination of Both

- How to Use People-Based or Place-Based Approaches Effectively

- Methods to Find Entrepreneurs Through Snowball Techniques and Support Organizations

- How to Maintain a Clear, Organized View of Who You Are Serving

Introduction

Chapter 7 introduced an organized approach to problem-solving using the Discover, Define, Develop, and Do framework. This chapter takes a closer look at the Discovery phase by focusing on how you locate and connect with entrepreneurs in your community. Before building relevant programs, you need to know who you are serving. The goal is to learn directly from founders, whether they operate a high-tech startup, a Main Street shop, or a neighborhood service, to gather authentic insights about their challenges, goals, and resource needs.

Identifying Target Entrepreneurs

Although you can try supporting all entrepreneurs at once, focusing your resources on a specific subset makes it easier to start strong. By making your efforts more targeted, you can deliver a clear, tailored set of support options that produce early wins. Later, you can expand or adjust this scope once you have built momentum.

Four Ways to Narrow Your Focus

- People-Based Approach: This method targets a demographic group, such as women entrepreneurs, youth-run businesses, immigrant founders, or veterans. It allows you to design specialized support around cultural factors, language, financial barriers, or networking preferences.

- Place-Based Approach: In this model, you prioritize a geographic location, such as a neighborhood, commercial corridor, city district, or rural region. You shape efforts around local resources, zoning, and community identity. For example, improving a specific block's business environment can become a pilot project for the rest of the city.

- Combined Approach: This option overlaps demographic and geographic considerations, such as focusing on Latina business owners in a certain neighborhood. It provides a high level of specificity but can also limit the number of participants, so make sure you have enough people to form a strong cohort.

- Matrix Approach: Suppose your community has enough data or a larger entrepreneurial population. In that case, you can map out different segments, such as industry type versus business stage, and then decide which box of that matrix to target first. This method is more complex but can reveal overlooked groups.

When selecting your focus, ask which segment needs the most support and matches your available resources. Also, check for an obvious gap, such as no existing programs serving that group or region.

Finding Your Entrepreneurs

Once you know which segment you plan to engage, you have to figure out how to locate them. A variety of methods will help you create a well-rounded list of contacts.

The Snowball Method

You begin with one or two entrepreneurs you already know, then ask for referrals. Each referral leads to another founder who can offer more connections. This approach works best when:

- You keep track of every contact to avoid double-counting or missing follow-ups.

- You reach out quickly to new referrals so you do not lose momentum.

- You move beyond your initial network to meet founders from different backgrounds.

Working with Support Organizations

Local chambers of commerce, business incubators, and small business development centers maintain lists of participants, alumni, or program clients. They may have a membership roster, a mailing list of past attendees, or data about who recently completed a training session.

- Lists and Directories: These might come from membership groups, city permit data, or local loan recipients.

- Data Sharing: Make sure you clarify privacy rules. Some organizations only share aggregated or partial data to protect confidentiality.

- Collaborations: Working with these organizations on outreach can lead to events that draw more diverse participants, such as a joint workshop or meet-and-greet session.

Alternative Finding Methods

- Drive-By Approach: Physically survey a target area to see which businesses exist. This helps you identify smaller, under-the-radar operations that might not appear in formal databases.

- Online Searches and Social Media: Look for local business listings or social media groups where entrepreneurs gather to exchange advice or promotions.

- University Partnerships: Colleges often track spinout companies, student-run ventures, or local alumni who started businesses. Researchers or professors might be eager to help connect you.

Managing Information

Gathering data from multiple sources can quickly become disorganized if you do not plan. Early on, create a simple database or spreadsheet where you log each entrepreneur's name, contact details, business type, and how you discovered them.

- Stay Consistent: Use the same labels or tags for categories like industry, years in business, or location so you can sort and filter easily.

- Note Potential Overlaps: Record if an entrepreneur appears on multiple lists. It may mean the person is highly engaged and worth interviewing for deeper insights.

- Protect Privacy: If you collect detailed information, especially about finances or personal stories, be transparent about how it will be stored or shared, and follow any local regulations on data privacy.

Engaging Entrepreneurs

Finding entrepreneurs is only the beginning. You need to reach out effectively so they see value in responding and sharing their experiences. Chapter 9 explores methods like interviews, focus groups, and surveys in more detail, but keep these general guidelines in mind:

- Make It Convenient: Schedule meetups or calls at times that suit business owners, often outside peak operating hours.

- Explain the Purpose: Entrepreneurs want to know how your research or initiative will help them.

- Build Trust: Respect confidentiality and follow through on any promises, such as sharing summary findings or connecting them with a relevant mentor.

Conclusion

Identifying entrepreneurs is a critical stage in the Discovery process of ecosystem building. By focusing on the right groups, using practical methods to locate them, and handling their information responsibly, you lay the groundwork for programs that fit actual local needs. In the following chapters, you will see how to gather deeper data from these founders and incorporate that knowledge into a meaningful plan to strengthen your community's entrepreneurial landscape.

For More See Toolkit 8: Entrepreneur Outreach Planner
It helps you plan and coordinate efforts to locate and engage the right segments of founders.

CHAPTER 9

DISCOVERY – QUALITATIVE

Chapter Roadmap

In this chapter, you will learn:

- Why Qualitative Data Is Vital for Understanding the Real Needs and Motivations of Entrepreneurs

- How to Conduct Focus Groups and Interviews Effectively

- When to Use Surveys for Broad but Less Detailed Insights

- Ways to Manage the Information You Gather to Keep It Organized and Secure

- How to Apply Qualitative Findings in Your Overall Ecosystem-Building Process

Introduction

Chapter 8 discussed how to identify and locate entrepreneurs in your community. Once you know who they are, you need a clear understanding of their experiences, needs, and goals. Qualitative data, information captured through conversation, observation, or open-ended questionnaires, adds depth to the broader picture you are forming in the Discovery phase.

While quantitative data is also important (as you will see in Chapter 10), it does not always capture the nuances of real-world experiences. Interviews, focus groups, and surveys help you tap into founders' personal stories and perspectives. By combining these insights with the strategic framework introduced in earlier chapters, you can make well-informed decisions serving the entrepreneurs at your ecosystem's heart.

Gathering Insights

Focus Groups

A focus group is a structured discussion with a small group of entrepreneurs who share their experiences, challenges, and ideas. By listening to each other, participants often uncover common themes or spark new ways of thinking about local obstacles.

Best Practices

- Keep groups between 6 and 10 participants so everyone can be heard.

- Use open-ended questions like, "What is the biggest hurdle you face in scaling your business?"

- Record the session or have a note-taker capture key points.

- Create a comfortable environment so participants feel safe sharing candid feedback.

Focus groups provide more direct interaction than surveys, which can lead to deeper insights. However, you must plan carefully to balance strong voices with quieter participants and ensure the discussion remains on topic.

Interviews

One-on-one interviews enable you to explore sensitive or detailed topics that may not arise in a group setting. These can be done in person, by phone, or via video call. Questions often start broadly, such as "Tell me about your business," and then follow the conversation wherever important issues or opportunities appear.

Best Practices

- Prepare a short list of priority questions, but remain flexible.

- Let the entrepreneur speak freely without interruption, then use probing questions to clarify or go deeper.

- Respect confidentiality. Obtain permission if you plan to record the interview or quote the entrepreneur publicly.

Interviews require more time, but they give you a personal window into the founder's mindset. These personal narratives can reveal complex barriers, like bureaucratic red tape or struggle with cultural assumptions, that general data might miss.

Surveys

Surveys are efficient for reaching larger groups. They can confirm trends in focus groups or interviews and help you discover how many individuals share certain views or challenges.

Best Practices

- Keep surveys concise, ideally under 10 minutes.

- Mix question types: multiple choice for quick stats, open-ended for richer insights.

- Distribute surveys through several channels, such as email lists, social media, or partner organizations that regularly communicate with entrepreneurs.

Surveys lack the depth of in-person conversation, but they reveal patterns across broader segments. They are most effective when used alongside face-to-face qualitative methods.

Advantages and Disadvantages of Each Qualitative Method

Focus Groups

- Advantages: Encourage interactive conversation and share insights quickly.

- Disadvantages: They require skilled facilitation, and a small group size may not represent the entire community.

Interviews

- Advantages: Allow deeper exploration of sensitive or personal topics.

- Disadvantages: Time-intensive data can be harder to compare across multiple interviews.

Surveys

- Advantages: Can reach larger numbers and provide quantifiable patterns.

- Disadvantages: Limited depth and risk of low response rates if poorly timed or promoted.

Managing Information and Confidentiality

When collecting qualitative data, it is important to maintain ethical standards and ensure participants trust you with their stories. Some entrepreneurs share highly sensitive details about financial or personal struggles.

1. Organize and Label: Keep a consistent labeling system for your notes, recordings, or transcripts to trace them accurately to each session.

2. Protect Privacy: Store files in a secure location and avoid sharing identifying information publicly unless you have explicit permission.

3. Communicate Your Intent: Explain how you plan to use the data. If entrepreneurs know their comments may help shape new programs or policies, they are more likely to open up.

Chapter 8 addressed the importance of an organized database for entrepreneur contacts, and you can integrate your qualitative findings into that system by linking each contact to notes or transcripts from any conversations you have held.

Conclusion

Qualitative data offers a close-up view of your community's entrepreneurial challenges and hopes. By running focus groups, conducting interviews, and distributing carefully crafted surveys, you capture stories and perspectives that clarify which resources and services will be most valuable. Managing that information responsibly ensures the ecosystem's trust and sets a solid foundation for the next phase, in which you will delve into quantitative metrics. The combined view from both qualitative and quantitative angles leads to action steps that resonate with local entrepreneurs.

For More See

Toolkit 1: Focus Group Preparation Checklist

Guides you in scheduling, facilitating, and capturing insights from focus groups.

Toolkit 2: Survey and Interview Guide

Explains how to design surveys and conduct interviews for deeper understanding.

Toolkit 4: Qualitative Data Analysis Tips

Shows how to interpret transcripts and open-ended responses, ensuring your data leads to actionable conclusions.

CHAPTER 10

DISCOVERY – QUANTITATIVE DATA

Chapter Roadmap

In this chapter, you will learn:

- Why Quantitative Data Adds a Vital Layer to Your Discovery Process

- Where to Find Relevant Data Sources in Government Reports, Commercial Databases, and Local Records

- How to Organize This Information So It Is Easy to Analyze

- Ways to Combine Numerical Insights with Qualitative Findings

- Which Actions Might Result from Key Trends You Identify

Introduction

Chapter 9 outlined how focus groups, interviews, and surveys yield important personal insights from entrepreneurs. While these stories are essential, numerical data can confirm the scope of the issues that arise in conversation. Gathering statistics and measurable indicators of local business activity lets you see if qualitative findings align with broader trends.

Quantitative data might reveal, for instance, that although many local founders mentioned trouble securing loans, data from lenders shows a high loan denial rate for certain groups or neighborhoods. These sorts of patterns help direct your efforts. In this chapter, you will learn where to find reliable data, how to handle it responsibly, and what to do once you have your results.

Where to Find Quantitative Data

Government Data

- National Agencies: The U.S. Census Bureau publishes County Business Patterns, which show how many businesses operate in each sector. The Bureau of Labor Statistics provides employment data, and the Small Business Administration may offer loan statistics.

- Local Entities: City and county offices often track business registrations, licensing, and permit approvals. They may also compile local economic reports with industry breakdowns, real estate trends, or demographic insights.

These sources provide baseline numbers that help you understand your region's economic structure and track changes over time.

Commercial Databases

Providers like Data Axle (formerly ReferenceUSA), Nielsen, or IBISWorld collate information about existing businesses, consumer demographics, and industry trends. Access can be expensive, but many libraries or universities offer free portals to these services.

- **Types of Data Available**
    - Contact details for local businesses
    - Market segment descriptions
    - Industry analysis or consumer spending data

Cross-referencing this information with your interviews or focus group notes can highlight untapped market niches or confirm that the local industry is growing.

Local Reports and Foundations

Groups like community foundations, regional nonprofits, or local advocacy organizations often publish their research. They might conduct needs assessments or produce annual reports highlighting business creation or funding challenges. While these documents can be more qualitative, many also include numerical data, such as the number of loans issued to new founders or the success rates of grant-funded programs.

National Surveys and Research Institutes

Sometimes, national nonprofits or research institutes, such as the Kauffman Foundation, publish entrepreneurship surveys that break down trends by city or region. These data sets can position your community's experiences within a broader context, showing whether a challenge is local or part of a broader issue.

Organizing and Analyzing Data

Collecting lots of statistics is not helpful unless you can keep track of what you have and turn it into usable information. Here are some ways to stay organized:

- Establish a Clear File System: If you download spreadsheets or PDFs, label them with the date and the source (for example, "Census_CountyPatterns_2023_Q1.xlsx").

- Use Simple Tools: Spreadsheet programs like Excel or Google Sheets let you filter, sort, and calculate. Basic pivot tables can help you spot patterns quickly.

- Create Data Categories: Group information by topic, such as demographics, business characteristics, funding, job creation, etc. This makes it easier to compare related metrics side by side.

Once organized, look for trends that align with the challenges entrepreneurs described qualitatively. If many founders mentioned difficulty finding retail space, does local property data show a shortage or high pricing? If so, your next steps might address commercial leasing issues.

Using Quantitative Data to Take Action

When combined with qualitative insights, statistics deepen your understanding. For instance:

- Spot Gaps: If you see that your region has an unusually low number of female-owned businesses, yet many focus group participants expressed interest in starting companies, you might propose targeted mentorship or funding programs.

- Address Policy: If data indicates that your city's licensing times are longer than average, you can bring this information to local officials to streamline the process.

- Measure Progress: Baseline numbers let you track improvements. If you know the current number of active startups, you can compare this figure after introducing a new incubator or loan fund.

By acting on the data's trends, you move past anecdotal evidence and shape stronger, evidence-based initiatives.

Conclusion

Quantitative data offers a valuable perspective on the scope and scale of local entrepreneurs' challenges. By using multiple sources, such as government reports, commercial databases, and local research, you form a factual backdrop to the personal narratives gathered in Chapter 9. Organizing your data helps you identify actionable insights rather than drowning in spreadsheets.

The best results appear when qualitative and quantitative insights work together, guiding you toward strategic changes that matter to founders. With your new understanding of both the human stories and the statistical realities, you are well-positioned to define priorities for the next phase of your ecosystem-building journey.

For More, See Toolkit 5: Quantitative Data Analysis Toolkit Provides steps for gathering local statistics, cleaning and analyzing them, and merging insights with qualitative findings.

CHAPTER 11

DISCOVER – UNDERSTANDING YOUR ECOSYSTEM

Chapter Roadmap

In this chapter, you will learn:

- Why Mapping Your Community's Resources Is Essential
- How Asset Mapping Catalogs and Clarifies Your Existing Supports
- How Ecosystem Mapping Goes Deeper by Highlighting Relationships and Connections
- Ways to Convert Basic Asset Maps into Entrepreneur-Centered Action Plans
- Methods to Integrate Both Approaches for a Dynamic View of Your Ecosystem

Introduction

Earlier chapters introduced the Discovery phase, including how to gather both qualitative and quantitative data about local founders.

This chapter takes that information further by showing how to visualize the entire entrepreneurial environment. Simply knowing which organizations and resources exist is not enough. Entrepreneurs often face hurdles when those resources remain uncoordinated or hard to navigate.

By mapping your local ecosystem, you learn how different elements interact, spot missing links, and see where collaboration can flourish. The aim is not just to list programs and spaces, but to recognize how entrepreneurs move among them. This leads to better coordination, clearer pathways, and stronger outcomes for the community.

Asset Mapping

Asset mapping is identifying and cataloging the resources that support entrepreneurs, such as coworking spaces, financial institutions, or community training providers. It also includes people with valuable expertise, from local mentors to retired professionals ready to share insights. The goal is to develop a comprehensive view of what exists and where it can be found.

Six Steps to Asset Mapping

1. Define Your Boundaries: Clarify the geographic area or community segment you will focus on.

2. Identify Partners: Bring in economic development agencies, chambers of commerce, and nonprofits that already track local resources.

3. Determine Asset Types: Group resources into categories like financial, infrastructural, knowledge, or support organizations.

4. List Group Assets: Gather details about banks, business incubators, training centers, etc.

5. List Individual Assets: Include mentors, business service providers, or specialized experts.

6. Create a Visual Map or Database: Please choose a format, maybe a spreadsheet, online platform, or printed directory, that makes it easy to see your community's resources at a glance.

Some communities start with a simple spreadsheet, labeling each row with the organization's name, type, services, and contact details. More advanced maps might feature an interactive website or a data visualization tool.

Ecosystem Mapping

While asset mapping lists and categorizes resources, ecosystem mapping examines the relationships between those resources. It also looks at how entrepreneurs navigate the support system. This approach highlights weak links or redundancies that can block progress.

Focus on the Six Domains

Chapter 1 discussed six core components of an entrepreneurial ecosystem: skills, relationships, finances, culture, policy, and infrastructure. Ecosystem mapping looks at how each component is present in your community and whether entrepreneurs can access it quickly and efficiently.

Connection Mapping

A key part of ecosystem mapping is identifying formal partnerships (like a memorandum of understanding between a bank and a community nonprofit) and informal ties (like a startup founder's personal connection to a local mentor). This helps you see who collaborates with whom, how resources flow, and where the biggest communication gaps lie.

When you overlay these relationships on top of your list of resources, you form a picture of how easy or challenging it is for founders to move between services, such as going from a business-planning workshop to a small loan application.

Converting Asset Maps to Entrepreneur-Centered Ecosystem Maps

A static list of resources does not show what entrepreneurs need at each step or where they become stuck. To make your map entrepreneur-centered, consider:

- Define Targeted Entrepreneurs: Chapter 8 explored whether you focus on youth founders, women entrepreneurs, rural communities, or some other specific group. Apply that focus to your map.

- Track Real Journeys: Interview or follow a handful of entrepreneurs to see which resources they used. Compare this to what is listed on your asset map. Often, some services remain overlooked.

- Add Informal Supports: Entrepreneurs might rely on family, cultural institutions, or local hangouts to find first customers or mentors. Incorporate these informal touchpoints in your map.

- Measure Connection Strength: Highlight which resources are heavily used versus those seldom accessed. If a particular service is highly effective, see if other assets can adopt similar practices.

By prioritizing the entrepreneur's viewpoint, you turn a standard asset map into a dynamic system that reveals where founders thrive or stumble.

The following is an example of U.S. Sourcelink's Resource Railway map of the local entrepreneurship ecosystem in Missouri. To learn more about their ecosystem mapping process, visit https://www.joinsourcelink.com.

Integrating Asset and Ecosystem Mapping

When done together, these two approaches form a complete picture:

- Asset Mapping tells you what resources exist, such as a small-business lending program or coworking space.

- Ecosystem Mapping shows how resources interact, how founders move among them, and where relationships need strengthening.

Steps to Combine Both

- Gather Data: Use your asset map as the starting list, then add arrows or lines that represent actual referrals, known partnerships, or frequently used pathways.

- Overlay Entrepreneur Journeys: Identify steps that are smooth and others that are bottlenecks.

- Find Gaps or Overlaps: Merging them might increase impact if two agencies offer the same workshop, but neither is widely attended. If a funding source is underused, perhaps the application process is poorly understood.

- Update Regularly: Because services, programs, and relationships shift over time, treat your map as a living document. Revisit and revise it at least quarterly or after significant program changes.

Conclusion

Understanding your ecosystem means more than compiling a directory of local organizations. It involves seeing how entrepreneurs engage with those resources, what connections empower them to grow quickly, and where the system leaves them searching. By combining asset mapping (the "who" and "what") with ecosystem mapping (the "how" and "why"), you can develop a strategic view of local entrepreneurship. This sets the stage for data-driven improvements, like new collaborations, policy adjustments, or redesigned support programs, that help founders bring their ideas to life and spark lasting community change.

For More See

Toolkit 6: Asset Mapping Template

Supplies a structured format for cataloging and visualizing local resources.

Toolkit 7: Resource List and Visual Examples

Offers references to data sources and illustration methods that enhance your ecosystem maps or presentations.

CHAPTER 12

BRIDGING INSIGHTS TO ACTION

Chapter Roadmap

In this chapter, you will learn:

- Why Synthesizing the Data You Gathered Matters for Informed Decision Making

- How to Use Structured Tools Like SWOT to Clarify Main Priorities

- Ways to Organize Your Findings So They Remain Actionable

- Why Sharing Discoveries with Stakeholders Increases Buy-In

- How to Transition from Understanding Your Ecosystem to Taking the Next Steps

Introduction

Chapters 8 through 11 explored how to discover important data about your community's entrepreneurs and ecosystem. You have likely conducted interviews, gathered surveys, reviewed local statistics, and mapped resources. This chapter consolidates those insights into clear priorities that will inform your next actions. Whether you are about to form a project team or propose new initiatives, you need a cohesive view of the challenges and opportunities revealed by your research.

By synthesizing your findings, you align stakeholders around common themes and set a focused agenda. You also allow yourself to confirm that your work so far addresses real needs. This process helps you identify where to invest time and resources and leads naturally to setting up the practical steps in the next phase of your ecosystem-building journey.

Synthesizing Insights

When you collect large amounts of information, such as focus group transcripts, survey data, and asset maps, it is easy for valuable details to get lost. Synthesis means combining all these pieces to find repeating patterns or especially urgent issues. By examining the data from different angles, you can confirm which elements best reflect the everyday experiences of local entrepreneurs.

1. Identify Patterns: Look for recurring barriers, such as lack of funding or complicated permit procedures. If multiple stakeholders mention the same problem, it deserves attention.

2. Connect Different Data Types: Merge your qualitative notes with your quantitative statistics. For instance, if your focus groups and local loan data show difficulty accessing small business capital, that gap is worth exploring.

3. List Gaps and Strengths: While it is easy to spot weaknesses, remember that existing strengths can act as

a foundation. These might include active volunteer mentors or a thriving downtown retail area.

Creating Clarity: Using SWOT Analysis

A SWOT analysis is a simple way to organize what you learn:

- Strengths: Qualities that give your community an advantage, such as affordable real estate or strong public support for local businesses.

- Weaknesses: Internal factors that make entrepreneurship more difficult, such as an outdated training curriculum or a lack of consistent networking events.

- Opportunities: External openings you can capitalize on, like a new federal grant aimed at business expansion or an industry trend favoring local sourcing.

- Threats: External risks undermine economic stability, such as a shrinking population or major job losses.

Classifying your findings into these four categories reveals where you can focus your efforts to maintain momentum or correct course.

Likely Ecosystem Assets Identified

By now, you have documented a variety of resources that can serve as pillars for new initiatives. These might include:

- Human Resources: Retired executives willing to mentor, teachers who coach student entrepreneurs, and civic advocates who support new policies

- Financial Resources: Local microloan funds, community foundation grants, or private investors looking to boost economic development

- Infrastructure and Spaces: A shared workspace in a repurposed warehouse, libraries or schools that host after-hours training, and technology labs open to the public

- Policy Support: Lawmakers aiming to streamline licensing, local ordinances that incentivize startups, or matching grants for broadband expansion

These documented assets help you decide where to build and how to avoid duplicating existing services.

Organizing and Documenting Findings

Categories and Tags

Group similar information under headings such as Access to Capital, Mentorship, and Infrastructure Gaps, then use consistent tags to make sorting and searching more efficient later.

Source Tracking

Log the origin of each piece of data, such as a focus group quote, a survey response, or a local government report. This step improves credibility and allows you to revisit sources when fine-tuning your priorities.

Timelines

Note when data was collected. Comparing information across different months or years helps you see whether issues are improving or remaining stagnant.

Sharing Findings

Before finalizing your plans, discuss your summarized findings with relevant stakeholders so that everyone can confirm the priorities. Presenting data also helps build trust.

- Presentations or Workshops: Host a brief meeting highlighting the core findings and explaining how they point to specific solutions.

- Concise Reports: Craft summaries highlighting what was found, why it matters, and how you plan to address it. A short document with charts or tables can make the data more accessible.

- Online Platforms: Post a read-only spreadsheet or infographic on a shared drive or community website. This transparency can encourage feedback from a wider audience.

Encourage feedback from the group. They may spot missing details, share new insights, or align more fully with your conclusions.

Conclusion

Translating your Discovery phase insights into an action plan requires weaving qualitative and quantitative data into a single narrative. Tools such as SWOT and strategic documentation ensure you recognize the strengths to build on and the gaps to fill. By engaging others in reviewing this information, you gain broader buy-in and a clearer roadmap for the next stages.

With this structured understanding, you are ready to progress from simply identifying entrepreneurial needs to launching initiatives that can address them. The chapters ahead explain how to build teams, manage timelines, and create effective projects that respond to the discoveries you have so carefully assembled.

For More See Toolkit 3: SWOT Implementation Worksheet It helps you transform gathered data into clear priorities and next steps by sorting them into strengths, weaknesses, opportunities, and threats.

ECOSYSTEM BUILDING TACTICS

"The best way to get started is to quit talking and begin doing." - Walt Disney

Having explored core concepts (Part I) and established a strategic foundation (Part II), you are now ready to implement your plans. Part III highlights hands-on tactics that move beyond high-level ideas into on-the-ground execution. You will learn to build effective teams, design key initiatives, and apply proven methods that keep your progress dynamic and visible.

This section walks you through the critical steps to make sure your ecosystem-building work becomes a tangible reality:

- Chapter 13: Building Your Team

  Focuses on how to gather diverse stakeholders, set clear roles, and foster collaboration. Explains ways to secure real resource commitments, such as time, money, or professional services.

- Chapter 14: Developing Your First Project

  Explains the Strategic Doing methodology, helping you translate ideas into a concrete plan with immediate wins and measurable outcomes. It covers brainstorming, prioritizing, and taking bold yet manageable first steps.

- Chapter 15: Exponential Ecosystem Growth

  Discusses methods for scaling successes by forming new teams that tackle additional ecosystem challenges. Shows how each group can build on existing knowledge while maintaining cohesion.

- Chapter 16: Building Forward

  Wraps up the journey with strategies for sustaining momentum, scaling impact, and ensuring your ecosystem remains open to fresh ideas. Guides you toward long-term resilience and community-wide transformation.

By following the principles and tactics in Part III, your ecosystem will move from a well-researched plan to a series of tangible projects that bring meaningful improvements to local founders and the broader community.

CHAPTER 13

BUILDING YOUR TEAM

Chapter Roadmap

In this chapter, you will learn:

- Why a Committed Team Provides the Backbone of Your Ecosystem Effort

- How to Engage Both Traditional and Non-Traditional Stakeholders

- Ways to Create Clear Roles, Responsibilities, and Expectations

- How to Secure Resource Commitments from Team Members

- Strategies to Maintain Motivation and Long-Term Dedication

Introduction

Chapters 8 through 12 explored various ways to discover your community's entrepreneurial strengths and challenges. You now have a clearer view of local founders, resources, and key data. The next step is putting that knowledge into action. Doing so requires a focused and collaborative team. These people will translate insights into tangible projects, form partnerships, and sustain momentum.

This chapter explains how to form a group that can serve as the core of your ecosystem-building efforts. You will also learn strategies for engaging their time and skills, so they move beyond occasional meetings to active ownership of your initiatives.

Assembling the Core Team

Team Composition

A strong ecosystem team blends different kinds of expertise and perspectives. Traditional stakeholders often include local business owners, bankers, municipal staff, and educators. Non-traditional stakeholders, such as faith leaders, community activists, or representatives from local arts groups, bring a wider view of community needs.

Aim for 8 to 10 people who can commit to several months of active involvement. Smaller teams may lack the range of skills needed for complex projects, and larger ones often struggle to coordinate effectively. Whatever the size, ensure that members share a passion for fostering entrepreneurship.

Key Team Characteristics

- Deep Collaboration: Members regularly participate, share resources, and plan together. Open communication fosters trust and synergy.

- Resource Allocation: Each member must bring time, funding, facilities, or networks that help launch real actions.

- Long-Term Commitment: This may mean attending monthly sessions, overseeing specific project tasks, and adjusting plans as new information emerges.

Making the Ask

Setting Expectations

Before you invite a prospective member, outline what is involved. This includes:

- Time commitments per month

- Responsibilities or decision-making roles

- Potential resource contributions (financial or otherwise)

When people understand the scope, they can decide whether they can commit. Clear expectations reduce misunderstandings and strengthen trust.

Commitment of Resources

Encourage future team members to think about what they can offer beyond attendance. This might include their network of professional contacts, specialized knowledge, event spaces they manage, or digital tools they know well.

If they say yes, confirm the details:

- How much time can they give each month?

- Which resources can they guarantee?

- Who from their organization might also participate?

Document these commitments, even informally, so everyone knows their role in moving the ecosystem work forward.

Developing and Keeping Your Team Engaged

Strategies for Team Engagement

- Clearly Define Roles: Assign tasks so each member knows their contribution, such as "outreach coordinator," "event planner," or "data manager."

- Gradually Increase Responsibilities: Give small, manageable tasks at first so people gain confidence.

- Provide Decision-Making Authority: Let team members shape the direction of the work. Shared ownership keeps them motivated.

Maintaining Commitment

Ecosystem building often spans many months or years. Keep people energized with:

- Regular Communication: A short monthly update that highlights progress, acknowledges success, and notes upcoming deadlines

- Visible Results: Show the effect of recent efforts, whether it is a new mentorship pilot or a successful networking event

- Recognition and Celebration: Publicly commend individuals who go above and beyond, and celebrate milestones as a group

A supportive environment helps team members remain passionate, even when challenges arise.

Conclusion

Building a capable and devoted team is critical in turning your ecosystem research into meaningful action. You lay a strong foundation by assembling individuals with diverse skills and backgrounds, defining expectations from the start, and consistently nurturing collaboration. In the next chapter, you will learn how to harness this team's efforts to design and execute your first major project, transforming ideas into tangible community-wide impact.

For More See Toolkit 10: Team Roles and Responsibilities It clarifies possible positions within an ecosystem group and how to allocate tasks so everyone stays on track.

CHAPTER 14

DEVELOPING YOUR FIRST PROJECT

Chapter Roadmap

In this chapter, you will learn:

- What Strategic Doing Is and How It Helps Launch Your First Project

- Why the Four Questions Guide You From Brainstorming to Execution

- How to Align Existing Community Assets With Your Project Goals

- Ways to Use the 2x2 Grid to Prioritize Initiatives

- How to Maintain Momentum After Initial Commitments Are Made

Introduction

Chapters 12 and 13 covered bridging insights into action and forming a capable team. Now, you are ready for a method to shape your first real project. Strategic Doing, which originated at Purdue University, offers an action-oriented framework for groups that lack formal hierarchies but share common goals. It emphasizes quick wins, measurable progress, and leveraging available resources.

This chapter introduces you to the four questions that power Strategic Doing: What could we do, what should we do, what will we do, and when will we meet again? You will see how these questions help you transform a list of possibilities into a concrete plan, complete with assigned tasks, clear timelines, and regular follow-ups.

Introduction to Strategic Doing

Strategic Doing arose from the idea that communities and networks must be flexible but organized when tackling complex challenges. Unlike traditional strategic planning, which can linger on big visions but slow down in execution, Strategic Doing focuses on immediate action and tangible outcomes.

It relies on short planning and review cycles, often 30 or 90 days. This approach keeps teams from getting stuck in endless discussions and promotes constant learning. Each cycle you complete builds trust among stakeholders, shows quick gains to encourage more buy-in and positions you to tackle bolder projects as your ecosystem grows.

The Core Principles

- Build on Existing Assets: Work with the resources, contacts, and expertise already present in your community.

- Link and Leverage: Form connections that multiply each participant's abilities. A shared event or codeveloped service can create more impact than separate efforts.

- Focus on Measurable Outcomes: Define metrics so you know whether your actions have meaningful results.

- Create Short-Term Wins: Show quick progress to maintain enthusiasm and keep the group on track.

The Four Questions

Strategic Doing uses a straightforward sequence of questions to guide the team from brainstorming to action.

1. What Could We Do?

Begin by brainstorming all possible initiatives addressing the key issues your earlier research identified. This is when you revisit the data, interviews, and maps to ensure your ideas align with real community needs. Encourage creative thinking. Do not dismiss an idea too early.

Key Tips

- Involve diverse stakeholders who bring different perspectives

- Reference your asset map to see which resources can be mobilized quickly

- Remember the people or areas you are targeting, such as women-led businesses or a specific neighborhood

2. What Should We Do?

Next, narrow your list using a 2x2 decision grid that evaluates each project by its potential impact and how difficult it is to implement. Label the grid with High vs. Low Impact on one axis and Easy vs. Hard on the other. Sort your ideas into these four categories:

- Easy / High Impact: Ideal for first projects because they offer clear results with minimal complexity

- Hard / High Impact: Ambitious efforts that you might plan for a later phase

- Easy / Low Impact: Quick wins that still help build team morale

- Hard / Low Impact: Likely to be dropped

The group should prioritize any ideas under Easy / High Impact that are strong candidates for your first major initiative.

3. What Will We Do?

Once you pick a priority project, set clear commitments within a specific time frame, such as 30 or 90 days. Assign tasks to individuals who have agreed to own them, and define what success looks like.

Example: If your chosen project is a monthly meetup for emerging entrepreneurs, you might commit to:

- Securing a free community space within two weeks

- Finalizing a list of potential speakers within three weeks

- Developing a simple website and social media announcement within one month

Clear deliverables and deadlines keep everyone accountable. Post these commitments in a shared location, such as a Google document or simple task manager, so that the group can review progress together.

4. When Will We Meet Again?

Schedule your next check-in before you conclude the current meeting. This ensures ongoing accountability and helps you handle any unexpected issues promptly.

Key Tips

- Monthly or bimonthly check-ins can work well

- Keep meetings concise. Focus on updates, challenges, and next steps

- Use a simple format, such as listing completed tasks, pending items, and any required course corrections

This regular cycle of planning, acting, and reviewing fosters a culture of action and transparency.

More About Strategic Doing

Strategic Doing is a peer-reviewed, scientifically grounded practice that teaches collaborative strategy in open networks. It provides a framework for groups to:

- Identify existing assets

- Develop strategies to leverage these assets into new opportunities

- Build trust through immediate implementation initiatives

You can explore the Strategic Doing Institute website or consider their practitioner training courses to learn more about Strategic Doing. The Strategic Doing Practitioner Training introduces you to the skills needed to:

- Enable teams to form action-oriented collaborations quickly

- Move toward measurable outcomes

- Make adjustments along the way

Visit: https://strategicdoing.net/a-brief-overview-of-strategic-doing/

Aligning Resources and Discovery Insights for Ideation

Before you begin, gather the data from your discovery phase and revisit which resources your team already controls. Knowing what your bank partners or local nonprofits can immediately offer helps ideas stay ambitious and realistic. By linking these assets with your top priorities, your group can move faster during the "what could we do" and "what should we do" phases, avoiding the pitfall of setting goals that require entirely new funding streams or programs.

Developing Your First Project

Use the Easy / High Impact ideas as your launchpad. Start small, prove the concept, and gather feedback from participants. Even if your bigger goals include large-scale changes like building a business incubator, you can begin by hosting a low-cost pilot program. Each success strengthens your team's credibility and draws more supporters.

Maintaining Momentum

Strategic Doing relies on short cycles and visible achievements to keep everyone engaged. At each review meeting, celebrate progress and solve problems that may arise. If you see strong results, consider expanding the project. If something is not working, adjust your approach without lengthy delays.

Regular communication between check-ins is also important. A brief email every couple of weeks can remind people of their commitments, update them on new partnerships, or ask for support if a team member encounters a roadblock.

Conclusion

By blending an immediate action mindset with a flexible, structured plan, Strategic Doing helps communities move quickly from brainstorming to tangible results. The four questions ensure that your ideas align with existing resources, have realistic priorities, establish clear responsibilities, and maintain regular follow-ups. With this framework, your first project becomes a concrete step toward building an entrepreneurship ecosystem that adapts to local needs and shows meaningful outcomes for everyone involved.

For More See Toolkit 9: Pilot Project Launch Planner Outlines how to organize, budget, and evaluate an initial project so you can learn quickly and refine your approach.

CHAPTER 15

EXPONENTIAL ECOSYSTEM GROWTH

Chapter Roadmap

In this chapter, you will learn:

- Why Team Multiplication Can Rapidly Expand Your Ecosystem Work

- How New Teams Form and Replicate Efforts Across Different Focus Areas

- Key Strategies to Sustain Quality While Scaling

- How to Address Resource Shortages or Communication Gaps in a Growing Network

- Ways to Measure the Long-Term Impact of an Expanding Team Structure

Introduction

Chapters 13 and 14 discussed building a dedicated stakeholder group and launching your first project. Although a single team can create valuable momentum, an entrepreneurial ecosystem often needs many groups working on different goals at once. This is where exponential growth, or team multiplication, comes into play.

In this chapter, you will see how new teams form and build upon the successes of the original team. Each group tackles its objective but shares knowledge and lessons with the others. Over time, this network of teams drives significant, community-wide change by handling multiple needs simultaneously.

Laying the Foundation for Rapid Growth

Success of the Initial Team

Your first group has already gone through planning and execution. They have discovered local needs, defined a workable project, developed the necessary resources, and carried out an initial program or event. This small success shows that action leads to tangible benefits for entrepreneurs, attracting more interest from community members.

That proof of concept is crucial. It gives new team members confidence that ecosystem building is not just talk. Documenting your processes and results, from meeting minutes to feedback forms, helps new groups hit the ground running. They can replicate and refine those strategies if they know how your founding team tackled issues.

The Multiplication Process

Exponential growth begins when experienced members from the first team step forward to lead newly formed groups. Instead of one team handling multiple large projects, new groups branch off and specialize in additional focus areas. For instance, if your first project improved access to mentors, a second team might zero in on funding opportunities, while a third addresses youth entrepreneurship.

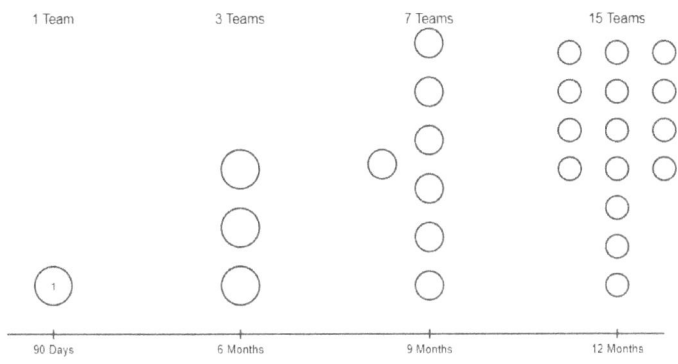

1 Team	3 Teams	7 Teams	15 Teams
90 Days	6 Months	9 Months	12 Months

How Teams Multiply

- Identify Multiplier Members: These are individuals with firsthand knowledge of ecosystem building who can guide others. Each new team they lead starts with 6 to 8 committed participants.

- Assign a Clear Goal: Each newly formed team chooses a specific outcome, based upon the prior insight gathered in the discover phase. This could be increasing small business loans or creating a peer networking community.

- Mentor and Collaborate: The original team continues its work and mentors new teams, sharing resources and contacts. This collective knowledge increases the odds of success.

- Build Cohesion: Regular cross-team check-ins ensure everyone can compare progress, address common challenges, and celebrate milestones together.

Specialization Over Time

As more teams form, some choose to specialize further. One group might focus on commercial corridors in underserved neighborhoods, while another focuses on advancing a tech cluster. This specialization helps the ecosystem cover many needs without spreading individual groups too thin.

Making Multiplication Work

Challenges of Growth

- Resource Shortages: Each new team needs leaders, funding, and time. Ensure you have enough human capital to guide multiple groups without burning out your original members.

- Communication Gaps: Confusion can arise about overlapping tasks or scheduling with many teams operating. Use simple dashboards and shared documents to keep everyone aligned.

- Maintaining Momentum: Without visible wins, teams may lose motivation. Encourage them to choose manageable tasks that yield results in a reasonable time frame.

Knowledge Transfer

Ensuring that new teams uphold consistent quality starts with effective knowledge sharing. This can include:

- Documentation: Keep a central repository of lesson plans, outreach methods, or workshop materials for easy reference.

- Learning Forums: Host monthly cross-team sessions so members can discuss both successes and pitfalls.

- Mentorship: Pair an experienced founder or program manager with each new group, providing real-time advice and troubleshooting.

When knowledge flows freely, teams avoid repeating mistakes and adopt proven best practices, accelerating the ecosystem's growth.

Coordinating the Expanded Network

A successful network of multiple teams needs some structure for alignment:

- Monthly Leader Meetings: Team leads share progress, plan joint activities, and request help if obstacles arise.

- Quarterly Gatherings: Larger events unite all teams to celebrate wins and discuss future directions.

- Shared Systems: Use a simple online platform to track outcomes, list resources, and record meeting notes. This transparency ensures no important detail is overlooked.

Conclusion

Exponential ecosystem growth hinges on multiplying teams that each address a different slice of your community's needs. By carefully documenting early successes, mentoring new groups, and maintaining open communication, you can expand your reach without losing focus. Over time, these multiple teams collaborate on specialized projects and amplify the overall impact. The final chapter will explore how to sustain and scale these efforts even further, ensuring that the momentum generated by team multiplication becomes a long-term force for local entrepreneurship.

For More See Toolkit 11: Multiplying Teams and Sustaining Growth
Details how to replicate and scale your successful initiatives across multiple teams, ensuring alignment and knowledge-sharing.

CHAPTER 16

BUILDING FORWARD

Chapter Roadmap

In this chapter, you will learn:

- How to Reflect on Your Ecosystem-Building Journey and Celebrate Progress

- Why Sustaining Momentum Requires Regular Evaluation and Flexible Strategies

- Ways to Scale Your Impact by Broadening Reach or Deepening Services

- How to Envision a Thriving Future for Your Community's Entrepreneurs

- Closing Thoughts for Those Committed to Long-Term Ecosystem Development

Introduction

Throughout this book, you have explored how to identify entrepreneurs, gather data, form effective teams, and put strategic actions into motion. You have also seen how those initial successes can multiply as new teams arise, each addressing a different area of need. This final chapter looks back on how far you have come and how to move forward, balancing sustainability and scalability.

A well-structured ecosystem supports entrepreneurs and brings broader benefits, such as revitalized neighborhoods, a stronger tax base, and more job opportunities for local residents. By continuing to adapt and expand, you ensure these benefits last and grow. This chapter explains how to maintain the energy you have built, continue scaling your efforts, and envision an optimistic future where entrepreneurship is woven into the fabric of your community.

Reflecting on the Journey

Recapping Key Principles

Your ecosystem building has followed a discovery, planning, implementation, and learning cycle. Key takeaways include:

- Prioritizing local leadership and collaboration

- Gathering insights from entrepreneurs through qualitative and quantitative methods

- Taking visible early steps to prove that real change is possible

- Documenting projects so new groups can replicate or refine them

Celebrating Progress

Encourage your team to pause and acknowledge the milestones you have reached, whether hosting a successful pilot program, securing grant funding, or increasing mentorship participation.

Small celebrations build morale, show the community that good work is happening, and attract more supporters.

Sustaining Momentum

Evaluate and Evolve

Check your efforts regularly to confirm they still match local priorities. Communities change, and new market trends can create different opportunities or challenges. You stay aware of entrepreneurs' current needs by conducting periodic focus groups, survey updates, or data reviews.

Institutionalize Knowledge

Preserve what you have learned in places others can find easily, such as a shared online folder or a brief annual report. This step prevents knowledge from disappearing when key individuals depart and allows new stakeholders to integrate quickly.

Foster Ongoing Collaboration

Keep relationships alive by continuing regular communications, such as monthly updates or quarterly gatherings. Encourage cross-team visits so each group remains aware of what the others are doing. Consider rotating leadership roles to share responsibility and freshen ideas.

Scaling Impact

Geographic Expansion

If you have succeeded in one neighborhood or district, consider replicating those methods in nearby regions. Remember to adapt to local differences. What worked downtown might require modifications for rural entrepreneurs or suburban business corridors.

Deepening Support

Rather than expanding geographically, you could deepen services in your original area. For example, add specialized mentorship or advanced tech training if you started with a microloan program. Adding layers of support enriches the ecosystem for those already involved.

Leveraging Partnerships

Connecting with regional or national organizations can boost your reach. They may offer funding, technical expertise, or a platform for sharing your successes with a wider audience. By collaborating with external partners, you can accelerate improvements without sacrificing the local character of your ecosystem.

A Vision for the Future

The ultimate goal of ecosystem building is creating a climate where entrepreneurship is normalized, diverse founders can thrive, and residents benefit from sustainable economic growth. Achieving that means:

- Supporting a consistent pipeline of new startups at all stages

- Removing structural barriers so more people can launch ventures

- Ensuring the community understands how local success stories help everyone

By embracing these elements, your community can lay the groundwork for continuous innovation. You empower local talent, keep wealth circulating within the region, and equip future generations to shape their economic destiny.

Closing Thoughts

Your journey has shown that entrepreneurship ecosystem building is a long-term commitment requiring collaboration, listening, and flexibility. The strategies and examples in this book are just the beginning. Keep learning, testing new ideas, and drawing on the power of shared efforts.

You can evolve a disconnected set of resources into a vibrant, transparent system by making small changes at each stage and never losing sight of local entrepreneurs' real needs. This system will help current founders succeed and inspire the next wave of innovators. With determination, open communication, and a belief in community-driven impact, you can build a future where entrepreneurship blossoms for everyone.

PART IV

TOOLKITS

"Do what you can, with what you have, where you are."
- Theodore Roosevelt

Parts I through III covered why ecosystems matter, how to gather and interpret data, and how to translate strategic plans into action. This final section offers practical resources to help you implement and maintain your initiatives. Each toolkit focuses on a specific aspect of ecosystem building, giving you tools to organize, train, and collaborate more effectively.

Toolkit 1: Focus Group Preparation Checklist

A step-by-step guide for planning and hosting focus groups, including sample questions, recruiting tips, and facilitation advice.

Toolkit 2: Survey and Interview Guide

Templates and strategies for designing surveys and conducting one-on-one interviews with local entrepreneurs, ensuring you capture reliable and meaningful information.

Toolkit 3: SWOT Implementation Worksheet

A fill-in-the-blank framework for translating your ecosystem's strengths, weaknesses, opportunities, and threats into focused action items.

Toolkit 4: Qualitative Data Analysis Tips

Suggestions for interpreting transcripts from interviews or focus groups, coding themes, and converting qualitative insights into actionable recommendations.

Toolkit 5: Quantitative Data Analysis Toolkit

Guidance on finding, sorting, and analyzing numerical data from local government reports, commercial databases, and community records. Offers tips on spotting trends and pairing them with qualitative findings.

Toolkit 6: Asset Mapping Template

A user-friendly layout for cataloging community resources and instructions for creating interactive maps or directories to link each resource to your broader ecosystem.

Toolkit 7: Resource List and Visual Examples

References to recommended books, research websites, and diagraming tools. Includes examples of how to present your data in clear, engaging formats.

Toolkit 8: Entrepreneur Outreach Planner

Helps you plan and coordinate efforts to identify, contact, and engage founders from specific demographics or geographic areas, complete with timelines and communication scripts.

Toolkit 9: Pilot Project Launch Planner

A blueprint for turning a small initiative into a working program. Covers budgeting, volunteer coordination, event logistics, and how to measure early outcomes.

Toolkit 10: Team Roles and Responsibilities

Defines potential roles within an ecosystem-building team, from project lead to data analyst. Offers strategies for delegation, accountability, and handling disagreements.

Toolkit 11: Multiplying Teams and Sustaining Growth

Explains how to replicate your successes across multiple teams, manage knowledge transfer, and stay aligned on shared goals as your network expands.

Use these toolkits to equip yourself and your partners for each step of the ecosystem-building process. By turning insights into actionable workflows and checklists, you can focus on delivering tangible results that strengthen local entrepreneurship.

FOCUS GROUP PREPARATION CHECKLIST

1. Define Your Purpose

- Clarify Your Goals: Know what questions or issues you want to explore. For example, you might want to understand financing barriers or test a new program idea.

- Identify the Audience: Decide which entrepreneurs to invite. You might focus on early-stage founders, a particular demographic, or operators in a specific industry.

2. Plan Logistics

- Choose a Date and Time: Consult your audience or use a quick poll to find a time that works for most entrepreneurs, such as early evening when shops have closed.

- Select a Location: Pick a neutral, easily accessible venue. Community centers, libraries, or coworking spaces often work well. If the session is virtual, decide on a reliable platform and confirm that participants can access the needed technology.

- Create a Budget: Factor in venue costs, refreshments, recording equipment, or small participant time incentives.

3. Recruit Participants

- Set a Target Group Size: Aim for 6 to 10 participants for manageable, in-depth discussions.

- Promote the Session: Use email lists, community bulletin boards, and social media. If you already have a contact database, send a brief invitation explaining the purpose and potential benefits.

- Follow Up: A week before the session, send a reminder with the date, time, and location or a virtual meeting link. Confirm final attendance numbers so you can prepare materials accordingly.

4. Develop Your Discussion Guide

- Outline Key Topics: Identify 3 to 5 main subject areas. For instance, you might explore financial challenges, available training, or needed mentorship.

- Draft Open-Ended Questions: Use prompts such as "Tell me about your biggest obstacle right now" or "How does the local community support your business?" Avoid leading questions that hint at a desired answer.

- Plan the Flow: Begin with easy warm-up questions to help participants feel comfortable. Move to deeper or more sensitive topics once rapport is built.

5. Set the Room and Materials

- Arrange Seating: Encourage eye contact by using a circle or U-shape layout. If virtual, advise participants to keep cameras on (if possible) for more natural engagement.

- Check Equipment: Beforehand, test recording devices, online meeting software, or presentation materials.

- Supplies: Provide name tags, pens, paper, and refreshments (if in person). In a virtual setting, share a digital file with the discussion prompts.

6. Facilitate the Session

- Establish Ground Rules: Explain confidentiality. Ask everyone to respect one another's viewpoints.

- Guide the Conversation: Focus on the main topics without quickly cutting off meaningful tangents. Gently bring quiet participants in and tactfully manage those who dominate.

- Capture Feedback: Record audio or take detailed notes. If using an online platform, ensure you save chat logs or transcripts.

7. Follow Up

- Thank Participants: Send a short email or message expressing appreciation. If you promised to share outcomes or notes, mention when they can expect them.

- Summarize Key Points: Review your recording or notes. Look for recurring themes, interesting quotes, and potential areas for further research.

- Plan Next Steps: Decide how to integrate findings into your broader ecosystem-building work. For instance, you might adjust a planned workshop or refine your mentorship program objectives.

Sample Questions

- "What is your biggest current challenge in running your business?"

- "Where do you usually go for advice or support?"

- "How would you describe the local culture toward entrepreneurs?"

- "If you could change one thing about doing business here, what would it be?"

This checklist helps gather meaningful data while ensuring entrepreneurs feel heard and respected. Following these steps will give you a deeper understanding of local needs, which you can then integrate into your strategic plans and ongoing initiatives.

SURVEY AND INTERVIEW GUIDE

1. Clarify Your Objectives

- Specify Your Goals: Know whether you want general feedback on available resources or detailed input on a new program.

- Define Your Audience: Determine if you target first-time founders, established business owners, or a particular demographic group.

2. Survey Preparation

- Determine Format: Decide if the survey is digital (email, social media) or paper-based. Online tools like Google Forms or SurveyMonkey can automate data collection.

- Keep It Concise: Surveys under 10 minutes get higher completion rates. Ask the essential questions first.

- Use a Variety of Question Types: Combine multiple-choice for quick stats, scales (1–5) for measuring opinions, and short open-ended boxes for nuanced feedback.

- Check for Clarity: Have a colleague or friend take the survey to spot confusing wording or overlapping answer choices.

Sample Survey Questions

1. Multiple Choice: "Which of the following funding methods have you explored?" (check all that apply)

2. Likert Scale: "On a scale of 1 to 5, how confident do you feel about accessing local mentorship services?"

3. Open-Ended: "What is your biggest challenge in growing your business right now?"

3. Survey Distribution

- Identify Channels: Email lists, online communities, or partner organizations can help you reach relevant entrepreneurs.

- Personalize Invitations: A short note explaining why you want their feedback often boosts response rates.

- Set a Deadline: Give participants a clear submission window (one or two weeks) and send one friendly reminder if needed.

4. Interview Preparation

- Choose Candidates: Decide on the number of interviews you can realistically conduct. Focus on a representative mix of entrepreneurs based on industry, tenure, and business size.

- Create an Interview Guide: Outline 5 to 10 open-ended questions, so you have a structure but can follow interesting tangents.

- Plan Logistics: Set up times that suit entrepreneurs' schedules. Decide if conversations will happen in person, by phone, or via video call.

Sample Interview Questions

1. Background: "Tell me about your journey to starting this business."

2. Challenges: "Which local resources, if any, helped you solve operational or financial issues?"

3. Suggestions: "How could community leaders better support founders like you?"

5. Conducting Interviews

- Begin with Rapport: Start by discussing something informal or referencing a positive fact about their business to ease into the conversation.

- Record with Permission: An audio recording or detailed notes let you revisit the dialogue accurately. Always ask for consent first.

- Listen Actively: Use follow-up questions like "Can you tell me more about that?" to encourage deeper reflection. Avoid interrupting.

- Watch for Non-Verbal Cues: Body language and tone can hint at how strongly someone feels about a topic, helping you focus on key points.

6. Analyzing Survey and Interview Data

- Organize Responses: If using an online platform, export results to a spreadsheet. Label notes by topic, such as Funding, Marketing, or Infrastructure, for interviews.

- Spot Trends: Look for recurring themes or barriers multiple participants mentioned and note differences across demographics or industries.

- Cross-Reference: Compare survey data with interview findings to see if the numbers confirm or contrast personal stories.

- Prioritize Action Items: For example, if many entrepreneurs cite limited coworking spaces, this might become a short-term goal to address.

7. Following Up

- Thank Participants: A short email or message shows appreciation and encourages ongoing goodwill.

- Share Key Insights: A summary of collective findings can motivate entrepreneurs who contributed to your research.

- Integrate Results: Feed these conclusions into your ecosystem planning efforts, whether revising a program idea, clarifying resource gaps, or adjusting timelines.

You gather quantitative and qualitative data by combining well-structured surveys with in-depth interviews. This approach enriches your understanding of local entrepreneurs, ensuring that your programs address real challenges and opportunities.

TOOLKIT 3

SWOT IMPLEMENTATION WORKSHEET

1. Clarify Your Purpose

- Define the Scope: Decide which part of your ecosystem to analyze, such as access to funding or mentorship support.

- Gather the Right Team: Include representatives from different sectors, like local government, entrepreneurs, banks, and educational institutions.

- Set Clear Objectives: Agree on why you are conducting the SWOT and how the results will be used.

2. Prepare Your Worksheet

- Create Four Boxes or Sections: Label them Strengths, Weaknesses, Opportunities, and Threats.

- Assign a Note-Taker: Have one person capture all ideas in each section.

- Provide Context: Briefly recap the data or observations you want participants to remember, such as survey results or interview highlights.

3. Identify Strengths

- Internal Qualities: List the attributes or resources your ecosystem already has, such as experienced mentors, enthusiastic civic leaders, or low living costs.

- Unique Capabilities: Note anything that gives you an edge, like a supportive business culture or an active local investors' group.

- Evidence: Encourage people to cite real examples. For instance, "Five local business owners volunteer as mentors" shows a tangible strength.

4. Identify Weaknesses

- Internal Limitations: These might be ineffective programs, limited outreach to certain groups, or outdated training resources.

- Current Barriers: Ask participants for practical examples, such as entrepreneurs lacking knowledge of available funding or unclear communication with existing service providers.

- Specify the Impact: Note how each weakness hinders ecosystem growth or discourages new founders.

5. Identify Opportunities

- External Openings: This might include a new state-level grant program for small businesses or an increase in remote workers looking for coworking spaces.

- Emerging Markets: Look for growing industries in your region, such as eco-friendly products or digital services, and note how you can nurture them.

- Trend Alignment: If local consumer preferences shift toward local vendors, highlight ways to boost marketing and awareness for community-based enterprises.

6. Identify Threats

- External Risks: Economic downturns, population decline, or major employers leaving the area.

- Competitive Pressures: Nearby cities offer better incentives or are experiencing a global shift away from certain industries.

- Regulatory Changes: New laws that might restrict certain business models or add complexity to licensing.

7. Prioritize Your Findings

- Ask, "Which Strengths Can We Leverage First?": A strong mentorship network could anchor a new incubator program.

- Ask, "Which Weaknesses Need Urgent Fixing?": A training workshop may be critical if a lack of financial literacy limits loan approvals.

- Rank Opportunities by Impact: A new grant might require an immediate application while forming a tech cluster might be a longer-term goal.

- Assess Threats by Severity: Decide which threats your ecosystem can handle with current resources and which require major changes.

8. Turn Insights into Action

- Assign Responsibilities: Write down which individual or team will address each priority.

- Create Timelines: Set immediate, short-term goals (1–3 months) and longer-term objectives (3–12 months).

- Measure Outcomes: Choose success indicators, such as the number of entrepreneurs trained or new partnerships formed.

Simple SWOT Table (Fill-in-the-Blank)

Strengths	Weaknesses
1. _____	1. _____
2. _____	2. _____
3. _____	3. _____
Opportunities	**Threats**
1. _____	1. _____
2. _____	2. _____
3. _____	3. _____

Fill in each section to complete your SWOT analysis

Use the above boxes to capture input from your group. Once you have filled them in, highlight the top items under each category and brainstorm how they connect. This exercise transforms raw observations into focused strategies that guide your next phase of ecosystem building.

QUALITATIVE DATA ANALYSIS TIPS

1. Organize Your Data

- Centralize Storage: Gather your transcripts, focus group notes, or open-ended survey answers in one place, such as a shared folder or spreadsheet.

- Label Carefully: Tag each document with clear identifiers (for example, "FocusGroup1_June2023" or "Interview_JohnD_Finance").

- Create a Tracking Sheet: Include columns for the participant's role, the session date, and the main topics covered to make filtering and sorting easier later on.

2. Familiarize Yourself with the Content

- Read or Listen Completely: Before you begin a detailed breakdown, quickly pass each transcript or recording to get a sense of the big picture.

- Take Preliminary Notes: Jot down recurring themes, surprising comments, or potential questions for follow-up.

3. Apply Basic Coding Approaches

- Highlight Key Sections: As you read more deeply, highlight words or phrases that relate to the focus of your study, such as "lacking mentorship," "confusing licensing," or "strong local support."

- Create Codes: Group similar ideas under short labels like "FundingBarrier," "MarketingHelp," or "PolicyIssues."

- Use a Simple System: You can code in a word processor by color-coding text or use a spreadsheet to note line numbers and categories. This step organizes raw data into more meaningful clusters.

4. Identify Patterns and Themes

- Consolidate Codes: Combine codes that are similar or overlapping. For example, "financial challenges" and "access to loans" might merge into one broader category called "FundingGaps."

- Spot Frequencies: Look for how often certain themes appear and which participants mention them. If multiple entrepreneurs cite a lack of networking opportunities, you may have found a priority to address.

- Search for Contradictions: Notice if different groups have conflicting views. If established business owners praise local support but newer founders do not, that signals a gap in awareness or outreach.

5. Triangulate with Other Data

- Compare Qualitative Codes with Survey Stats: If many participants say they struggle to find mentors, see if your quantitative survey also shows a high demand for mentorship programs.

- Check Asset Maps: Match references to "lack of coworking" with your mapped resources. Are there spaces entrepreneurs do not know about, or are they absent?

6. Summarize Findings

- Draft a Simple Report: Group your major themes into categories. Include short, direct quotes that highlight each point.

- Highlight Key Insights: Emphasize frequent patterns and any striking outliers that deserve attention.

- Point to Next Steps: End with recommended actions or questions that arose from the data. This helps transition into your broader ecosystem strategy.

7. Reflect and Share

- Validate with Stakeholders: Present highlights to your team or relevant leaders. Ask if the findings resonate with their experiences.

- Plan Further Research: If new questions emerge, decide whether you need additional interviews, focus groups, or a follow-up survey.

- Integrate into Action: Feed your qualitative conclusions into planning sessions for workshops, pilot projects, or policy suggestions.

By systematically coding and analyzing your qualitative data, you can identify patterns that show what entrepreneurs need. This structured approach ensures you do not overlook valuable feedback, guiding your ecosystem-building efforts toward programs and policies that resonate with local founders.

QUANTITATIVE DATA ANALYSIS TOOLKIT

1. Define Your Purpose

- Clearly state what you want to learn from your data, such as identifying growth industries or confirming a suspected gap in loan approvals.

- Be specific. For instance, decide whether you need current-year figures or a multi-year comparison to see trends over time.

2. Gather Data Sources

- Government Reports: Try the U.S. Census Bureau or Bureau of Labor Statistics for up-to-date population, employment, or business creation figures.

- Commercial Databases: Consider platforms like Data Axle (formerly ReferenceUSA) or IBISWorld, many of which are accessible through public libraries.

- Local Records: Tap into city or county databases for business permits, registrations, and funding distributions.

3. Organize Your Information

- Centralize Files: Keep all spreadsheets and PDF reports in one folder. For easy reference, use clear naming conventions (for example, "CityData_2022_Q2").

- Create a Master Spreadsheet: Combine relevant columns, such as business names, industries, and location data. Verify that headings and data formats are consistent to avoid errors.

4. Clean and Validate

- Remove Duplicates: Unify the record under one entry if the same business appears multiple times.

- Check Formats: Standardize categories like "Industry" or "Zip Code" so you can sort and filter effectively.

- Handle Missing Data: Document gaps and decide if they significantly affect your conclusions.

5. Analyze with Simple Tools

- Sort and Filter: Sort data by date or location to see if growth is concentrated in particular areas. Filter to isolate segments, such as businesses founded in the past year.

- AI Evaluation: Use an AI tool to group data by industry or business size to identify which categories are expanding. Look for anomalies like an unexpected spike or drop in a specific niche.

- Basic Calculations: Compute averages or percentages to gauge trends, such as the rate of new business starts each year or the proportion of female-owned enterprises.

6. Look for Patterns and Trends

- Compare Time Periods: If you suspect a decline in manufacturing startups, check figures from the last few years side by side.

- Cross-Reference Qualitative Insights: See if your numbers support common themes mentioned in interviews or focus groups. If many founders cite a lack of financing, do local bank records show fewer small-business loans?

7. Visualize Findings

- Create Simple Charts: Line graphs or bar charts can highlight year-over-year changes or differences across locations. Pie charts can show the distribution of industries in your region.

- Map Data: Consider using basic mapping tools to illustrate the density of businesses or resources in certain neighborhoods.

8. Communicate Outcomes

- Summarize in Plain Language: "Thirty percent of new business registrations in the county happen in just two zip codes," or "Only 15 percent of business loans go to startups less than two years old."

- Highlight Actionable Points: Suggest possible next steps, such as targeting an underrepresented industry or launching a mentorship program for businesses in certain areas.

9. Revisit Regularly

- Update Data: Decide whether you will pull fresh numbers monthly, quarterly, or annually. This keeps your ecosystem picture current.

- Share Updates with Stakeholders: Let them know when new figures are available, especially if they influence ongoing projects or partnership decisions.

This toolkit helps you transform raw statistics into meaningful insights for decision making. By systematically collecting, cleaning, and analyzing quantitative data, you can spot patterns that validate or challenge your qualitative findings, paving the way for evidence-based improvements in your community's entrepreneurial environment.

ASSET MAPPING TEMPLATE

1. Decide Your Scope

- Clarify the geographic area or demographic group you plan to serve. You might map a single neighborhood, city, or a countywide region.

- Define what assets you want to track, such as mentoring, funding, training spaces, or specialized services.

2. Choose a Format

- Spreadsheet or Database: Offers a list-based approach that is easy to sort and update.

- Visual Map: Tools like Google My Maps or diagraming software help you see relationships at a glance.

- Hybrid Model: You can maintain a master spreadsheet and create snapshots as visual diagrams for presentations.

3. Categorize Your Assets

- Common Categories: Mentorship, Financial Institutions, Educational Programs, Community Organizations, Physical

Spaces (such as incubators or coworking locations), and Policy or Government Support.

- Subcategories: If your community has many resources, consider subcategories like early-stage funding vs. expansion capital or technical advice vs. general business coaching.

4. Collect Your Information

- Tap Known Sources: Check local directories, government databases, and chamber of commerce listings.

- Interview Stakeholders: Ask entrepreneurs which resources they use or recommend. Personal references often uncover lesser-known supports.

- Note Key Details: Each entry should include contact info, main services offered, and special eligibility (for instance, women entrepreneurs or certain zip codes).

5. Organize and Verify

- Keep Entries Consistent: Use a standard naming convention and group entries by category so you can filter or search easily.

- Check Accuracy: Confirm addresses, phone numbers, and active links. Remove outdated entries or combine duplicates.

- Update Frequently: Community programs evolve, and new organizations appear. Plan a schedule to review and refresh your map.

6. Create Your Asset Map

- Spreadsheet Approach:

1. Make columns for Name, Category, Services, Contact, and Notes.

2. Highlight or color code entries that might overlap, like two incubators offering similar workshops.

- Visual Approach:

    1. Plot each resource on a map if location is important.

    2. Use icons or colors to differentiate categories (a green symbol for funding sources, a purple icon for coworking sites).

7. Look for Gaps and Connections

- Identify Duplicates: If multiple groups offer the same service, see if they can coordinate or merge efforts.

- Spot Missing Pieces: You might notice a shortage of advanced tech training or a lack of mentorships in a specific industry.

- Compare to Entrepreneur Feedback: If people say funding is a challenge, confirm whether funding institutions exist or if entrepreneurs are unaware of them.

8. Share and Update

- Make It Accessible: Post your map or spreadsheet on a shared drive, community website, or at local events, so entrepreneurs know where to look.

- Invite Corrections: Ask for feedback from organizations to correct or refine their listings.

- Document Changes: Whenever a service ends or a new one emerges, record the updated date so users trust the map's accuracy.

Simple Asset Map Example

Resource Name	Type	Contact Information	Services Provided	Connections
Local Bank	Financial	123-456-7890	Small business loans	Connects to incubators
Coworking Space A	Infrastructure	Email	Office space, networking events	Links to mentors
Tech Training Academy	Educational	Email	Coding bootcamps, workshops	Partnerships with schools
Chamber of Commerce	Support Org.	Email	Business promotion, advocacy	Collaborates with local businesses

This toolkit helps you produce an organized resource list that shows how your community's supports align and what might be missing. By visualizing where opportunities exist and where gaps remain, you can develop projects and partnerships that help more entrepreneurs access the help they need.

RESOURCE LIST AND VISUAL EXAMPLES

1. Helpful Websites and Tools

- Data and Research

  - U.S. Census Bureau (census.gov) for demographics and business patterns.

  - Bureau of Labor Statistics (bls.gov) for employment data and sector growth.

  - Data Axle (via many public libraries) for local business listings and expansions.

- Visualization Platforms

  - Google My Maps is used to plot community resources on a geographic map.

  - Miro is used to create flowcharts or network diagrams that illustrate relationships between support programs.

2. Sample Visual Formats

- Resource Map: Create a digital map with markers for each asset (bank, incubator, training center). Color-code markers by category, such as financial services or mentorship.

- Flowchart or Network Diagram: Show how entrepreneurs might progress from one resource to another. Arrows can represent referrals, while different node shapes indicate distinct service types.

- Simple Bar Charts or Pie Charts: Compare data like the number of founders by industry, the size of mentorship programs, or funding allocations across neighborhoods.

3. Tips for Adapting to Local Context

- Gather Key Variables: Decide which data is most relevant to highlight. For example, if your region emphasizes retail, more prominently, reflect that in your resource map.

- Keep Graphics Straightforward: Complex visuals can be confusing. Start with one clear objective, such as showing which neighborhoods offer the strongest financial support.

- Consider Your Audience: Officials may prefer numeric summaries, while entrepreneurs could benefit more from a clear map or infographic pinpointing available resources.

4. Updating and Sharing

- Maintain Version Control: Mark any updates with a date so users know which version they view.

- Encourage Feedback: Ask stakeholders to identify missing entries or offer corrections. This increases buy-in and data accuracy.

- Use Multiple Formats: Present a simple one-page summary at community meetings and offer a more detailed online map linking resource names and contact details.

By utilizing these online platforms and graphical approaches, you can present your ecosystem's information in a concise way that entrepreneurs and community members can navigate easily. This clarity helps everyone see where help is available and where gaps remain.

ENTREPRENEUR OUTREACH PLANNER

1. Define Your Objectives

- Clarify Your Goals: Decide whether you invite them to a workshop, build an ongoing network, or gather feedback on their challenges.

- Choose a Target Audience: Identify which demographic or industry segment you want to reach, such as first-time founders, female entrepreneurs, or tech-focused businesses.

2. Identify Potential Contacts

- Gather Existing Lists: Start with membership rosters from chambers of commerce or small business associations.

- Use Digital Tools: Search LinkedIn or online business directories for local founders in your focus area.

- Ask for Referrals: Apply the snowball method by asking each contact to recommend other entrepreneurs who may be interested.

3. Plan Your Timeline

- Set a Concrete Start Date: Pin down when you will begin sending out invitations or announcements.

- Schedule Reminders: Prepare short follow-ups to nudge entrepreneurs who have not responded.

- Allow Time for Preparation: If you plan a meet-and-greet or an event, give participants at least two weeks' notice.

4. Tailor Your Communication

- Draft a Clear Message: In one or two sentences, explain why you are reaching out. Show how entrepreneurs will benefit from connecting with your ecosystem.

- Choose Appropriate Channels: Email may work for established businesses, while text or social media might better reach younger founders.

- Personalize Where Possible: Mention a fact about their business or industry and express genuine interest in their challenges or successes.

5. Maintain Regular Follow-Up

- Log Interactions: Keep a short note of each conversation or response in a centralized spreadsheet or CRM system.

- Respond Promptly: Quickly reply to questions or meeting requests, which sets a positive tone and builds trust.

- Invite Continued Participation: Direct entrepreneurs to an upcoming workshop or an online community space where they can stay connected.

6. Track and Measure Success

- Set Metrics: For instance, how many new entrepreneurs you plan to contact, how many respond, or how many attend your events.

- Review Outcomes: Check whether your outreach brings in a good mix of participants every few weeks. If not, adjust your methods or message.

- Refine Over Time: Update your contact list as you learn more about who is most responsive or which outreach channel is best.

By following this outreach planner, you can systematically build relationships with local entrepreneurs. Clear objectives, consistent follow-ups, and genuine interest in their needs all help lay the groundwork for fruitful collaboration and long-term engagement with your ecosystem.

Industry and Size Matrix Example

Industry Category	Gig Worker	Micro-business	Mom & Pop	High-Growth
Technology (Software, AI, etc.)				
Manufacturing (Food production, advanced materials, etc.)				
Retail (Independent shops, online stores, etc.)				
Services (Healthcare, professional services, etc.)				
Tourism & Hospitality (Hotels, restaurants, attractions, etc.)				

Industry and Stage Matrix Example

Industry Category	Concept	Startup	Growth	Mature
Technology (Software, AI, etc.)				
Manufacturing (Food production, advanced materials, etc.)				
Retail (Independent shops, online stores, etc.)				
Services (Healthcare, professional services, etc.)				
Tourism & Hospitality (Hotels, restaurants, attractions, etc.)				

Demographic and Geographic Matrix Example

Demographic	Neighborhood	Zip Code	Area of City	City
Black Women				
Asian Women				
Native Women				
White Women				
Women				

PILOT PROJECT LAUNCH PLANNER

1. Start with Discover and Define

1. Clarify the Issue or Opportunity: Draw on your recent discovery data (focus groups, surveys, asset maps) to pinpoint one urgent need or promising idea. Create a concise problem statement or goal reflecting your team's shared understanding.

2. Refine the Scope and Success Criteria: Define success markers for your pilot. For instance, if you are piloting a mentorship program, a success marker might be signing up ten mentors and pairing each mentor with at least two entrepreneurs.

3. Check Available Resources: Use your asset map and team discussions to confirm which resources you already control (time, funding, space, or volunteer capacity). This step ensures you design a pilot that is ambitious yet realistic.

2. Ask: What Could We Do?

1. Brainstorm All Options: As part of the Strategic Doing "What could we do?" step, list every idea that might address the need. Do not rule out suggestions too quickly; encourage creativity.

2. Leverage Existing Assets: Review your discovered or mapped resources and see which can be mobilized immediately. This might include a free meeting space, a grant that covers training costs, or a partner eager to co-sponsor events.

3. Consider Timelines: Decide if you want a 30-day or 90-day project cycle. Shorter cycles help you learn quickly, adapt, and build momentum.

3. Narrow It Down: What Should We Do?

1. Use Quick Prioritization: Employ the 2x2 grid from Chapter 14 or a simple discussion to see which ideas are easy to launch and likely to produce high-impact early wins. Drop low-feasibility or low-value options.

2. Set a Clear Project: Once you pick your pilot, write a brief summary of its core goal. For example, "Host a two-month mentorship pilot that pairs local founders with experienced professionals."

3. Agree on Metrics: Decide how you will measure success. This might be tracking how many mentors and mentees join, how many sessions occur, or participant satisfaction scores at the end.

4. Commit: What Will We Do?

1. Break the Project into Milestones: Outline key steps (securing a venue, recruiting mentors, running sessions,

collecting feedback), assigning each step to a specific person or subgroup.

2. Assign Roles and Deadlines: Confirm who coordinates outreach, who manages logistics, and who handles data. Set realistic timelines for each milestone so your team can stay accountable.

3. Set a Short Review Cycle: Often teams use 30-day sprints. Plan a mid-cycle check-in to see how the project is unfolding and whether adjustments are needed.

5. Schedule the Next Check-In: When Will We Meet Again?

1. Plan Regular Updates For a 60- or 90-day pilot, schedule a monthly or biweekly meeting to review tasks, share progress, and address challenges.

2. Document Findings: If something is not working, pivot quickly rather than waiting for the pilot to end. Keep notes on each pivot, as these learnings inform future projects.

6. Launch and Track

1. Communicate the Start: Announce key dates and instructions for participants, mentors, or collaborators. Make sure everyone knows their tasks and next steps.

2. Monitor Data and Feedback: Collect quick observations from participants along the way. For example, if your pilot is a mentor-mentee program, ask how often they meet and whether they see value in the sessions.

3. Stay Adaptable: If you identify barriers (too few mentors or scheduling conflicts), address them immediately by adjusting your outreach or shifting meeting times.

7. Conclude and Evaluate

1. Compare Results to Goals: Review your initial metrics. If you aimed for 10 mentors but only got 6, note why. If satisfaction rates are high, consider how to keep that momentum going.

2. Gather Final Feedback: Invite participants to fill out a short post-project survey or attend a wrap-up session. Identify lessons they believe should be carried forward.

3. Decide Next Steps: If the pilot succeeded, scale it up. If it had mixed results, adapt the process or refine your concept. If it seems unfeasible, move on to a different idea, but keep the lessons documented for the future.

8. Share Outcomes

1. Present Data Publicly: Create a short, clear report of your pilot's achievements or obstacles. Show how it ties back to the broader ecosystem mission.

2. Archive Materials for Future Teams: Store checklists, meeting notes, participant feedback, and other relevant documents in a shared space so new teams can replicate or improve upon your pilot.

3. Celebrate Wins: Even small wins build morale. Thank collaborators, mentors, or attendees, and highlight early adopters who served as champions of the pilot.

TEAM ROLES AND RESPONSIBILITIES

1. Define the Team's Purpose

- Clarify Your Mission: Start by stating what your group wants to accomplish. For instance, the team might focus on creating a mentorship network or improving local funding access.

- Identify Key Tasks: List your major activities, such as organizing workshops, tracking data, or building partnerships.

2. Outline Core Roles

Below are common roles you might include. Adapt them to your specific needs or the size of your team.

Project Lead or Facilitator

- Keeps team discussions on track

- Manages the overall schedule and sets meeting agendas

- Coordinates with external partners or stakeholders when needed

Data and Research Coordinator

- Collects and analyzes relevant information, such as local business registrations or survey results

- Consolidates findings into summaries for the team

- Monitors progress and outcomes over time

Outreach and Communications Lead

- Handles public messaging (flyers, social media posts, email campaigns)

- Maintains relationships with community groups, event hosts, or the local press

- Builds and updates the contact list of entrepreneurs and mentors

Logistics or Operations Manager

- Secures venues, equipment, or catering for events

- Oversees budgets and tracks expenses

- Ensures materials, such as worksheets or name tags, are ready

Mentor or Subject-Matter Expert

- Offers specialized knowledge (for example, legal or accounting help)

- Guides program content or workshop topics

- Serves as a resource for team members and entrepreneurs

3. Assign Responsibilities

- Document Each Person's Role: Use a simple sheet or shared online file to note who holds which position and what tasks they cover.

- Set Expectations for Time Commitments: If you need 5 hours per week from the Outreach Lead, clarify that upfront. This minimizes surprises or unbalanced workloads.

4. Foster Accountability

- Create a Task List: Break down larger goals into smaller tasks with clearly stated owners and due dates.

- Use a Tracking Tool: A shared spreadsheet or project management app helps the team see at a glance which tasks are pending, in progress, or done.

- Schedule Check-Ins: Decide how often to meet or send status updates. Some teams hold a brief weekly call, and others do monthly recaps by email.

5. Manage Conflict and Overlap

- Be Transparent: Encourage open communication if members feel they are doing tasks outside their role or see inefficiencies in the structure.

- Reassign or Redistribute: If someone has too many tasks, lighten their load by dividing responsibilities among others.

- Clarify Decision-Making: Agree on who has the final say for certain types of issues, such as budget approvals or scheduling large events.

6. Evolve the Team Structure

- Review Roles Periodically: As the project scales or your focus changes, you may need new positions or to combine existing ones.

- Invite New Members: Bringing in fresh volunteers or subject-matter experts can spark new ideas.

- Document Lessons Learned: Keep notes on what role setups worked best. This helps future teams form quickly and avoid repeating mistakes.

By defining roles and responsibilities from the start, your team avoids duplication of effort and ensures that everyone works in harmony. This intentional structure also helps each member feel valued and see exactly how their work advances the larger mission of building a stronger entrepreneurial ecosystem.

MULTIPLYING TEAMS AND SUSTAINING GROWTH

1. Assess Your Initial Success

- Document Early Wins: Record what your first team accomplished, such as hosting a successful workshop or filling a known resource gap.

- Identify Core Lessons: Note which strategies worked, which did not, and what you would do differently next time. This helps new teams avoid re-learning the same lessons.

2. Choose Multiplier Members

- Look for Experienced Leaders: Select individuals from your original team who grasp the project details and your overarching mission.

- Set Expectations: Make sure they are willing to mentor new groups, share templates, and maintain consistent communication.

- Balance Workload: Ensure these members are not overstretched. If they cannot commit the time, recruit others, or spread responsibilities among several people.

3. Form the New Teams

- Define Clear Goals: Each new group should have a focused objective, whether that is creating a mentorship network, developing a coworking space, or addressing an industry gap.

- Recruit Members: Pull from different backgrounds to encourage varied perspectives. Seek entrepreneurs, service providers, and possibly local officials like your original team.

- Structure at the Outset: Decide how often the new teams meet, whether they will use a shared tool for collaboration, and how they handle reporting.

4. Knowledge Sharing and Alignment

- Create a Shared Repository: Use a central space (like a Google Drive or a simple web portal) where documents, meeting notes, and templates are posted.

- Host Monthly Leader Calls: Bring team leaders together to trade insights, discuss common hurdles, and propose combined efforts (for example, a joint outreach event).

- Standardize Procedures: Ensure each group uses a consistent process for volunteer recruitment, budgeting, or communications tasks. This uniformity makes cross-team collaboration smoother.

5. Mentor and Guide

- Offer Ongoing Support: Multiplier members should be accessible for questions from the new teams, especially in the early weeks of setup.

- Encourage Adaptation: Let each group modify templates to suit their focus or local context but remain available to troubleshoot any major changes.

- Review Progress: Regularly check that the new teams meet their milestones and stay aligned with the bigger ecosystem goals.

6. Handle Scalability Challenges

- Resource Allocation: If multiple teams need funding or volunteer hours, clarify how to distribute these fairly.

- Communication Gaps: As teams multiply, the chance for miscommunication grows. Use shared trackers or dashboards to minimize confusion.

- Conflict Resolution: Encourage teams to raise issues promptly, whether about overlapping events or differing visions, and assign a neutral mediator if needed.

7. Sustain Momentum

- Publicize Wins: Celebrate each new team's achievements, whether a first pilot event or a new partnership. Sharing success stories motivates everyone.

- Plan for Growth: More teams may form if your network does well. Decide if there is a point at which you shift to a more formal structure (for example, an advisory board or a coordinating council).

- Monitor Long-Term Impact: Collect metrics over time, such as the number of new businesses launched, or the funds distributed to entrepreneurs, so you see how the entire ecosystem improves.

8. Evaluate and Improve

- Set Review Cycles: Schedule a collective review (every 6 or 12 months) for all teams to present outcomes and discuss adaptations.

- Document Changes: If a team merges with another or splits into two specialized groups, track that development and update your shared resources.

- Refine Toolkit Materials: Every new round of team-building will surface lessons. Keep all documents current so the next wave of teams can benefit from your ongoing experience.

By following this process, you can spread effective practices across multiple teams without losing the principles or structures that made your first effort successful. Over time, these groups form a network that addresses multiple ecosystem gaps in parallel and propels your community forward as a hub of entrepreneurship.

ADDITIONAL READING

"Entrepreneurship Ecosystem Building Playbook 3.0" (Kauffman Foundation, 2019)
This practical guide outlines principles and recommended actions for building inclusive entrepreneurship ecosystems, drawing on extensive insights from ecosystem builders in the United States. It describes collaborative strategies to unite diverse stakeholders and defines goals for expanding opportunities.
https://www.kauffman.org/ecosystem-playbook-draft-3/

"Future of Cities: A Roadmap to Inclusive Entrepreneurship" (National League of Cities, 2022)
It shows how entrepreneurship can be an engine for economic security and wealth-building while acknowledging the systemic challenges underrepresented founders face. Emphasizes that city leaders play a central role in addressing inequities, closing the digital divide, and enabling marginalized entrepreneurs to thrive.
https://www.nlc.org/resource/future-of-cities-a-roadmap-to-inclusive-entrepreneurship/

"Entreprencurchip Ecosystems in Appalachia" (Appalachian Regional Commission, 2018)
Focuses on the unique challenges and opportunities for ecosystem builders across the Appalachian region. Provides actionable recommendations and real-world examples for strengthening entrepreneurship support in rural communities.

https://www.arc.gov/report/entrepreneurial-ecosystems-in-appalachia/

"Local Entrepreneurial Ecosystems Toolkit"

This toolkit outlines five essential elements of a healthy entrepreneurial ecosystem, explaining why a new economic development approach is needed and providing detailed chapters on each element, including explanations, implementation activities, resources, and success stories. After describing the complete framework, it offers a simple roadmap for communities to build upon their existing entrepreneurship ecosystem, along with practical tools for implementation.

https://cameonetwork.org/wp-content/uploads/2019/11/CAMEO-LEEP-white-paper-2019.pdf

"Energizing Entrepreneurial Ecosystems: A Practitioner's Guide" (e2 Entrepreneurial Ecosystems, 2021)
Focuses on supporting homegrown business development in smaller communities. Highlights ways to mobilize local leadership, strengthen networks, and build equity into ecosystem strategies.
https://www.energizingentrepreneurs.org/library/entrepreneurial-ecosystem-building-strategies.html

"Entrepreneurial Ecosystem Diagnostic Toolkit" (Aspen Institute, 2013)
A toolkit based upon historical models of how to examine and evaluate entrepreneurship ecosystems.
https://www.aspeninstitute.org/wp-content/uploads/files/content/docs/pubs/FINAL%20Ecosystem%20Toolkit%20Draft_print%20version.pdf

Key Books

***Startup Communities: Building an Entrepreneurial Ecosystem in Your City* (2nd Edition) – Brad Feld (2020)**
Using the Boulder Thesis as a guiding framework explains how startup communities form and thrive. Includes examples of

successful hubs and methods to keep entrepreneurs engaged over time.
Purchase:
https://www.amazon.com/dp/1119617650

Beyond Collisions: How to Build Your Entrepreneurial Infrastructure – **Maria Meyers & Kate Pope Hodel (2017)**

Argues for creating community-driven support structures so aspiring business owners can succeed. It covers developing mentorship pipelines, coordinating resources, and replacing "silver bullet" solutions with lasting cooperation.
Purchase:
https://www.amazon.com/dp/0692999892

Ecosystems Emerge – **Dell Gines (2022)**

Examines entrepreneurship ecosystem building as a modern economic development practice, contrasting it with older industrial attraction models. Explains how to promote local business growth through collaborative, community-led initiatives and critiques various approaches to development.
Purchase:
https://www.amazon.com/Ecosystems-Emerge-CEcD-Dell-Gines/dp/B09RG1GQQ3

Additional Books

Energizing Entrepreneurs: Charting a Course for **Rural Communities – Deborah Markley, Don Macke, Vicki Luther (2005)**

Explores how rural leaders can invigorate local entrepreneurship, offering practical advice, real-world stories, and tested methods for creating a supportive environment.
Purchase:
https://www.amazon.com/gp/product/0974702722/ref=as_li_tl?ie=UTF8&camp=1789&creative=9325&creativeASIN=0974702722&linkCode=as2&tag=ryanlillycons-20&linkId=96114cb210d75d3319d1af31787a63ef

Notable Articles and Additional Reports (U.S. Authors)

"Grow Your Own: Entrepreneurship-Based Economic Development for Local Communities" – Dell Gines (Federal Reserve Bank of Kansas City, 2015)
Explains how communities can shift from recruiting external firms to developing their own businesses, with practical guidance on supporting small, local founders.
https://www.kansascityfed.org/documents/299/gyo-entrepreneurship-econ-dev-local-communities.pdf

"Building Inclusive Entrepreneurship Ecosystems in Communities of Color" – Dell Gines & Rodney Sampson (2019)
Presents a metrics-based approach for fostering high-growth entrepreneurship in underrepresented communities. Highlights ways to ensure equity across programs and resources.
https://metadataetc.org/gigontology/pdf/Building%20Entrepreneurship%20Ecosystems%20In%20Communities%20of%20Color.pdf

"Now More Than Ever We Need Ecosystem Builders" – Jeff Bennett (2020)
Makes a case for community-driven ecosystem builders and their importance in economic recovery. Argues that a supportive, system-wide approach helps founders succeed, especially during periods of uncertainty.
View Article:
https://startupsac.com/now-more-than-ever-we-need-ecosystem-builders/

These references offer a deeper knowledge of entrepreneurship ecosystems, from national-scale reports to practical how-to guides. They focus on diverse regions and approaches, showing how thoughtful collaboration and equity-centered strategies can advance local economic potential for all.

GLOSSARY

Asset Mapping
A process for identifying and organizing the resources available to entrepreneurs in a community. This might include physical spaces, funding sources, mentors, and training programs.

Bottom-up Action
Local initiatives driven by community members rather than external organizations. People who know the community best lead these efforts to meet real needs.

Connection Density
The number and strength of relationships in an entrepreneurship ecosystem. High connection density usually means entrepreneurs find resources and partners more easily.

Discover, Define, Develop, Do (4D) Framework
A structured method that guides you from understanding a problem to implementing a solution. In ecosystem building, it helps teams move from research to real results.

Early Wins
Initial successes that quickly show value. They build momentum, demonstrate feasibility, and motivate stakeholders to stay engaged.

Ecosystem Builder
An individual or organization that actively works to unify resources, create partnerships, and support entrepreneurs. They look for gaps, manage projects, and encourage a culture of collaboration.

Ecosystem Mapping
A way to visualize how different elements of an entrepreneurial

environment connect. It goes beyond listing resources by showing how they interact and influence each other.

Environmental Assets
External factors such as culture, infrastructure, and policy that shape how easily entrepreneurs can start and grow businesses.

Exponential Growth
A pattern of ecosystem expansion where multiple new teams or groups form based on the lessons and successes of an initial team, resulting in a rapid increase in impact.

Focus Groups
Small group discussions designed to gather qualitative insights about challenges, needs, or opinions. Entrepreneurs share experiences and often discover common ground.

Knowledge Transfer
The practice of systematically sharing data, skills, and best practices across teams or organizations. This ensures new groups benefit from the successes and avoid the mistakes of previous efforts.

Multiplier Members
Individuals from an existing team who start new teams. They share knowledge and lessons learned, making it easier for new groups to succeed.

Personal Assets
Characteristics or resources that belong to the entrepreneur, such as skills, finances, and personal networks. They combine with environmental factors to determine success.

Resource Flow
The movement of funding, materials, knowledge, or support across different players in the ecosystem. It is important for filling gaps and avoiding duplication.

Snowball Method
A technique for finding entrepreneurs by asking each contact to

refer you to additional contacts, allowing you to build a larger list of potential participants.

Strategic Doing
An action-oriented approach for decentralized networks. It revolves around four key questions to move from brainstorming to execution, emphasizing short cycles and measurable outcomes.

Support Organizations
Entities that help entrepreneurs, such as chambers of commerce, accelerators, mentorship groups, and nonprofits. They offer education, connections, or financial resources.

SWOT Analysis
A tool for evaluating Strengths, Weaknesses, Opportunities, and Threats. It helps you organize insights and identify priority areas for action.

Systems Thinking
A perspective that looks at how different parts of a community or process interact. It reminds us to consider how changes in one part of the ecosystem affect the whole.

Team Multiplication
A process where the successes of one ecosystem-building team inspire the formation of additional teams. Each new group addresses specific needs, expanding the overall impact.

Traditional Stakeholders
Established organizations and individuals often associated with economic development, such as banks, government agencies, educational institutions, and business leaders.

2x2 Grid
A decision-making tool that classifies ideas or projects into four quadrants: high or low impact, and easy or hard to implement. It helps groups prioritize which initiatives to tackle first.

.

www.ingramcontent.com/pod-product-compliance
Lightning Source LLC
Chambersburg PA
CBHW071840200326
41519CB00016B/4186